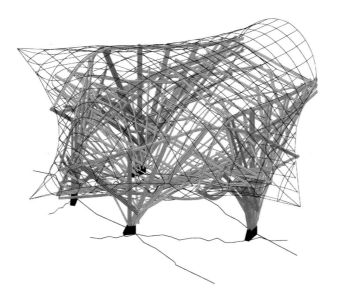

THE ECOLOGICAL HOUSE

WHITE STAR PUBLISHERS

THE ECOLOGICAL HOUSE

SUSTAINABLE ARCHITECTURE AROUND THE WORLD

preface
ecosistema urbano

text
marco moro
beatrice spirandelli

editorial project
valeria manferto de fabianis

editorial staff
federica romagnoli

graphic design
maria cucchi

CONTENTS

---

1 Model of the bamboo cupola at the Ecological Children's Activity Center (Soneva Kiri Resort, Koh Kood, Thailand).

2-3 Carmarthen Place (London, United Kingdom).

4-5 Villa Lena (Espoo, Finland).

6-7 Wisa Wooden Design Hotel (Helsinki, Finland).

9 Big Dig House (Lexington, Massachusetts, USA).

11-12 Study for one of the urban catalyst buildings – concentrators of activity and dynamizers for the urban scene – from the project by Ecosistema Urbano for filling vacant lots in urban neighborhoods in Philadelphia.

14-15 Palmyra House (Nandgaon, India).

PREFACE by Ecosistema Urbano

José Luis Vallejo, Belinda Tato, Michael Moradiellos, Domenico Di Siena

The 21st century is confronted with multiple and convulsive changes, as well as with crises – energy, food, water, economy, society – that impact every aspect of our lives and that will even further influence those of future generations.

This situation, whic≤h affects the entire planet, requires us to develop great creativity to approach the emerging problems from a new perspective.

History demonstrates how humankind has progressively adapted itself by creatively finding solutions to the various environmental problems people have had to face from time to time. It is interesting to learn how different cultures faced similar problems, and whether they were able to overcome them.

The time has come to produce greater knowledge in the field of architecture, and to promote diffusion of those projects and initiatives that represent adequate responses to a given environment, or which investigate and experiment with new technical solutions in the search for greater efficiency.

Education, information, and work are essential if we hope to glimpse a way out of our predicament rather than surrender to boundless, paralyzing pessimism.

In an era in which knowledge is free and accessible, information can be gathered in real time from any place, and technology allows us to work peer-to-peer. It is now possible for millions of people to cooperate on a global level toward the formation of a complex neuronal framework that makes our common resources and knowledge available for the good of all.

Elinor Ostrom, winner of the 2009 Nobel Memorial Prize in Economic Sciences in 2009, dedicated years to the study of self-organizing economic models, in order to demonstrate that common goods – commons – can be administered effectively by groups of users. Ostrom studied how human beings interact with the goal of long-range maintenance of production levels for the existing common resources (forests and hydrological resources, including fishing and irrigation systems, grazing lands, and so forth).

By contrast with the traditional view of economists, who consider it possible to maintain such resources only through state intervention or privatization, Ostrom affirms that the users of common goods develop sophisticated decision-making mechanisms and sets of rules for managing conflicts of interest, which lead to positive results that are often better than those predicted by the most highly accredited theories.

Ostrom's objective is to create a formal general system allowing identification and study of the elements and variables that influence the possibility of self-organization by communities in relation to the development of sustainable socioecological constraints.

A world without codes, where knowledge flows freely, will tend to minimize inequalities, by multiplying and favoring acceleration of sharing of information in the search for solutions promoting human well-being and a balanced relationship with the environment.

In this context, the architect must apply his creativity toward glimpsing new professional opportunities, and toward defining a new social role that is more coherent with the current scenario.

What would happen if, as in the field of open-source software, anyone and everyone could use, copy, study, change, realize, distribute, or modify the projects published here?

What outlooks could be foreseen from the promotion of a network system of projects – on the basis of free usage licenses – to developtechnical solutions generated collectively and in a nonprofit context?

Might not a book such as this one allow the selected projects to constitute a database available for future hypotheses of work, thus optimizing the individual efforts of dozens of architects?

We are facing great challenges. We need to imagine new economic scenarios based on interchange and interaction. We live in an exciting time for architecture and creativity.

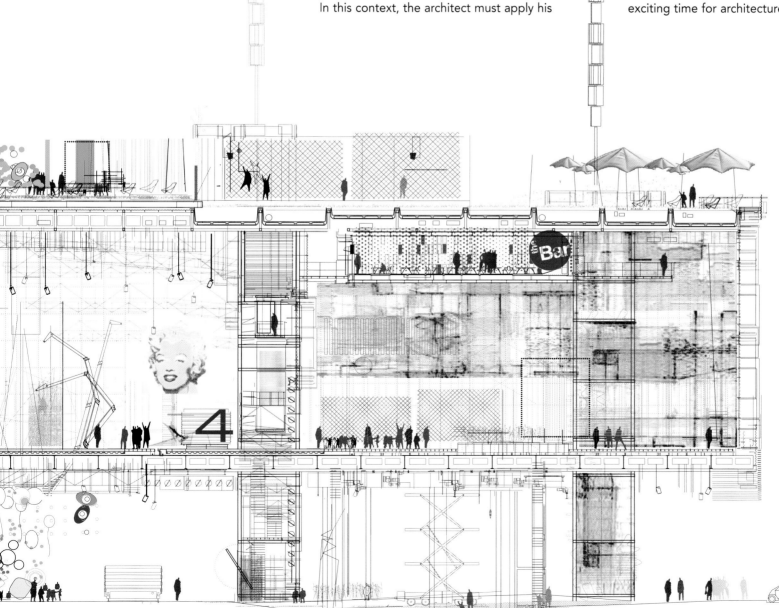

INTRODUCTION

The turning point came only recentlya recent one. It occurred in 2008, when, for the first time in the history of our civilization, the population living in cities exceeded that living outside them. The single-family home is still the most widespread form of dwelling today, but the rising and unstoppable urbanization of the world population could finally transform this reality that once seemed inevitable. What is actually going on? And according to what time frame? It is difficult to say because population does not transfer to urban centers in an orderly manner. Metropolises undergoing convulsive, uncontrolled growth are offset by cities and regions in decline, inexorably losing inhabitants, or cities that see their populations progressively moving toward suburban areas, emptying the historic nuclei.

The driving forces of the change are to be sought in the fluctuations of the global economy, factors that are not easy to connect intuitively to the way people live and how their houses are conceived and realized.

And the growth of the city does not always signify an increasing propensity for, or possibility of, living in multiple-family buildings, or perhaps in innovative emerging facilities such as cohousing communities. A good part of this expansion of the cities still requires single-family homes. The dwellings in the boundless slums that strongly characterize urban growth in Third World countries and certain emerging economies are also "single-family."

There is, however, one unifying piece of data; in fact it is the theme to which this volume is dedicated: the emerging of the interest in, and the necessity for, a different way of constructing and inhabiting our living space. It is the affirmation – on a truly global level – of the theme of the ecological house, which today comprises a fascinating repertory of proposals, expressions, and solutions for single-person or single-family dwellings. A repertory that is becoming ever broader, to the point that the selection of architectural works presented in this volume should be understood as only a small sample of the diverse various possibilities. In order not to render this a repetitive or useless exercise, or to mimic an already desperate, encyclopedic effort, we have highlighted new orientations of the project planning culture; new experiments with constructional techniques, materials, technologies, and architectural languages; new demands on the part of clients (or in other words, the new "public taste"); and, finally, new places to add to the already vast atlas of ecological and sustainable architecture.

This latter element recurs in all popular works that aim to give an identity to a cultural tendency: documenting how a way of construction is spreading on an international level is useful for certifying its credibility and success. This is what happened, for example, with the Modern Architecture movement. In our case, however, the operation is complex. There is not a stylistic unity that serves as a guide in the search for examples, or that visually testifies to the authenticity of what has been affirmed above; there are no international conferences, like the CIAM, where rules and orientations are fixed; there is not (and perhaps there cannot be) an Athens Charter for sustainable architecture. Because each individual project, by itself, makes history. And it is with this perspective that we measure the profoundness of an evolution that is even now in full development, involving not only the profession of project designer, but also the culture of the commissioners, the skills of the builders and artisans, and the technological innovation on the part of the producers of materials, components, and technologies.

At most, if we actually want to go searching for recognizable "styles," we could find a few traces on just a local scale. And this introduces another fundamental factor: diversity is a of the characteristic of ecological or sustainable architecture.

As in any ecosystem – – where biodiversity is the true wealth and best guarantee of vitality – the great diversity of approaches, languages, and material and technical cultures characterizing the architectural works presented in this book testifies to the rooting and, in fact, the vitality of a phenomenon that represents a substantial paradigm shift.

Is no doubt risky to draw a parallel between living systems and the world of architecture, but it is useful to propose certain fixed points. Without overflowing into territory that is still largely unexplored regarding techniques of biomimesis, ecological houses are planned on the basis of criteria that make frequent reference to the processes of nature. In the first place, nature does not waste. There is no rubbish. In the second place, each form of life is the result of adaptation to specific environmental conditions. In the third place, this adaptation means developing the capacity to best exploit the conditions of the given context.

These considerations – it must be emphasized – are also a pretext for determining a line of reading, of deciphering the extremely vast repertory of examples that are available today. These have led us to select and group the projects into three different sections, plus one smaller section, a quasi-appendix.

A first group of house projects was selected on the basis of their capacity to give new significance to the concept of the relationship between an architectural work and its context, whether natural or artificially constructed. This relationship takes into consideration all the elements which define the characteristics of the site: not only the natural ones (climate, air, soil, intensity of solar radiation, presence of vegetation, and so forth), but also those that are anthropic in origin, and therefore also cultural and social.

A second grouping presents examples of houses that successfully reduce waste and, more generally, reduce consumption of energy, materials, and space. Saving energy, intensive (or even just intelligent) use of space, recycling materials, recovery of entire buildings – these are the answers.

The third group of projects enters more into the details of what we have defined as the biodiversity of building, by analyzing the material aspects of ecological architecture: structures, shells, partitions, finishing. The world of natural materials appears in all its wealth – wood, earth, stone, straw, together with many other more unusual materials (from hemp to bamboo) – to constitute the "natural menu" from which the project planner can make selections.

Lastly, one of the pivot points of this new culture of ecological and sustainable construction and living is attention toward the psycho-physical well-being of the inhabitants. The last brief section dedicated to tourist facilities places particular emphasis on this aspect: hotels, vacation homes and resorts are the places for temporary lodging coinciding, for the most part, with the time when people give the greatest attention to their own well-being: travel time and vacation time.

Naturally, and we will reassert this often, the majority of the houses presented in this volume could be included in any one of the three sections. Buildings that have a highly calibrated relationship with their surroundings are, almost inevitably, also works of architecture that do not waste (space, energy, materials) and that arrive at this result also by mindfully using renewable, locally available resources. At times, it required a real effort to decide which section a given project fit best. But even this is one of the specific characteristics of the sustainable project planning approach. Even if it is not always holistic, at any rate it takes into account a number of variables and factors that are much broader than what we could define as the ordinary or conventional project approach.

The question we could pose at this point is: does the perfect ecological house exist? Perhaps. Among the many examples included in this volume are a few credible candidates for the title. The pleasure of discovering them is left to the curiosity of the reader. But this is not the point. The point is that the single-family home, even if constructed with all the requisites that could make it into an exemplary "ecological" dwelling, will never be perfect in reality. Its handicap is density: there are too few residentsguests" in a single-family home per square meter of occupied ground space by comparison with nearly all other residential typologies. Consumption of ground space, the shrewdness needed in considering its utilization, the quality needed to transform it into living space: these themes are the order of the day, especially in more densely populated contexts.

At an architectural Biennale of a few years ago, the Belgian pavilion presented a setup dealing with this very theme that produced a great impact. Titled Floating Islands, the exhibition pointed the finger at the consequences of the Belgians' excessive love for the single-family home, prefabricated and chosen from a catalog if possible. Naturally, the whole thing has obvious negative implications: besides there being less work for the architects – which is no legitimate complaint for anyone – there is a problem, seriously, of quality of space. The dissemination of single-family homes in the territory of agglomerations is a process that not only wastes space, but also leads to the formation of disproportionate suburban areas. These areas are not city, not village, not countryside, not even periphery. They are suburbia, a space without connective fabric, produced by the mechanical positioning of individual little homes, lot after lot, onto the terrain.

Having said this, the fact remains that, as we mentioned at the beginning, dwelling in a single-family home is not only a lifestyle that is shared by many, but also a desire and an objective that even now is very widespread, not only among the Belgians. Urban sprawl, the term commonly used to indicate the spreading of artificially constructed portions over a territory, is not a phrase of Flemish or French origin.

In conclusion, if the future of the single-family home may appear uncertain, at least in part, its present situation is doubtlessly characterized by a high level of innovation and creativity in project planning, making it fascinating and exciting for us to perform the research needed formulating to select the projects presented on these pages. M.M.

glenn murcutt *(the marika-alderton hous* *(residência na barra do sahy)* - olavi kopc *(house of steel and wood)* - emma dohe place) - zen architects *(north carlton gree* *(palmyra house)* - andrade morettin iguchi *(camouflaged house 3)* - dock4 untertrifaller architekten *(haus A)* - *ville CK06)* - baumraum *(copper cube)*.

belonging to a place

) - nitsche arquitetos associados
nen *(villa lena)* - ecosistema urbano
ty & amanda menage *(carmarthen*
house) - studio mumbai architects
arquitetos *(residência RR)* - hiroshi
rchitecture *(bull bay house)* - dietrich
pablo katz architecture *(maison de*

belonging to a place

"Usually the construction of new houses is synonymous with desecration and coincides with the birth of neighborhoods less attractive than the countryside they are built upon (... In spite of the bitterness of this equation, we generally accept it, with passiveness and resignation ... Accordingly, in regard to the skyscraper, to the new village in style, or to the villa on the river, we avoid posing the opportune question, most elementary and irritating: 'Who did all this?'"

In fact, who is it that constructs the landscape? What are the forces, the driving factors? Who dictates the rules? Who, materially, determines the appearance of the places where we live? What are their cultures, their interests?

Alain de Botton, philosopher and author of the quotation above (taken from The Architecture of Happiness, Pantheon Books, 2006) concludes: "An urban settlement that destroys some 40 km (about 25 mi) of countryside will be the work of certain individuals who were not particularly unholy or evil. They might be called Derek or Malcolm, Hubert or Shigeru; they might like to play golf or love animals ..." Ordinary people who, however, in a short time put into motion a process that determines the appearance of the place for centuries.

If each new construction that settles into a territory is commonly viewed today as an act of violence, or at best a worsening of the existing situation, what is the way out? Even the best of ecological houses cannot, evidently, do anything to reverse those processes of consumption of ground space and transformation of territory that are triggered and determined on a scale that, for the most part, has nothing to do with that of the project of an individual building.

The disenchantment and ill temper with which we observe, especially in more developed countries, the addition of a new neighborhood, a new shopping mall, an nth parceling of lots, as well as the results of the large-scale speculative operations inside the city, ought to be directed toward that sphere – highly opaque for the city dweller – where decisions are made to define the transformations that our environment will undergo.

This does not absolve project planners, who often are quite present even at those decision-making levels, in the padded rooms of power, where what we as residents perceive as the physical scenario of our life becomes something similar to a Monopoly board.

But it is just this condition, this difficult role of intermediary between investors' intentions and the object of such intentions – the environment (built upon or not) – that has offered architects the possibility of elaborating responses, to refine strategies to prevent the trauma of transformation from becoming an injury inflicted upon the territory. By designing houses that, in various ways and from various points of view, attempt to formulate a new idea of belonging to a place, a relationship with the environment, to be understood in the broadest possible sense: as a physical, social, cultural environment.

The houses presented in the following chapter – and many others, as well, in the various sections of this volume – present diverse views of relationship with a given context, by indicating possibilities of concrete action. How?

The first point is to relate to the constructional tradition of the place, to its techniques and materials, which are, for the most part, those that are locally available, materials whose performance has long been proved and translated into ways constructing that respond best to the specific environmental characteristics.

What architects like Helmut Dietrich and Much Untertrifaller, as well as the entire group of baukünstler from Vorarlberg in Austria, have realized is exemplary from this point of view: recovering the constructional culture of the place, innovating with it from top to bottom, relaunching it, and at the same time distilling formal and distributive solutions more adequate to its requirements and to contemporary languages. The same sensitivity for the constructional culture of the site can be found in various Australian projects, illuminated by the work of Glenn Murcutt, who succeeded even in redeeming a poor material – traditional, though, in rural contexts on that continent – like corrugated steel. The Madrid studio Ecosistema Urbano succeeds in combining various archetypes of the constructional culture of the region of the Asturias, deriving from it a model of ecological living that is fully contemporary. Other extraordinary examples of relationship with the constructional culture of a given site, as previously mentioned, can be found in other sections of the book.

It is worth mentioning the house on Lake Maggiore, by Italian architect Pietro Carmine, now deceased, a true example of fusion between architecture, local culture, and landscape. Integration of the construction into the landscape is one of the principal qualities of Olavi Koponen's architectural works. This assumes almost symbolic merit in "objects" like Camouflaged House 3 by Hiroshi Iguchi, or the house among the trees by baumraum.

The other large work context is the relationship between physical characteristics and local climate. In this sense, the works of Andrade Morettin Arquitetos and of Nitsche Arquitetos Associados in Brazil are among the most fascinating: light shells, totally open to a natural environment of great value, and in response to a perennially warm and humid climate, such as that of the Mata Atlantica. These elements appear also in the Palmyra House by Studio Mumbai Architects in India, realized with nearly maniacal attention, not only to environmental data, but also to all of the "presences" to be found in the terrain upon which the house was built, united with a profound respect for the available artisanal knowledge, which the architects endeavored to revitalize and showcase.

These many and various possibilities are by no means precluded from working in an urban setting, as demonstrated by the house at Carmarthen Place in London, which successfully redefines its context, above and beyond the lot it was built upon; or the North Carlton Green House in Melbourne, realized on a terrain of only 166 sq m (about 1785 sq ft), but finding the space and manner to relate to the surrounding landscape.

Brenda and Robert Dale, the two English architects famous for their theory of the "autonomous house" (and, obviously, for having realized several of them) in their recent book, Time to Eat the Dog? (Thames and Hudson, 2009) open the chapter dedicated to sustainable living with a meaningful "No Buildings" warning. Many current constructions, the authors sustain, reflect no true necessity, whether functional or cultural. There are too many of them, and too often they are useless. And meaningless. Where can we begin to rebuild a sense for today's architecture? From what point can we attempt to start anew, to make it once again acceptable, and accepted? Safeguarding of the place is the first and fundamental step to be completed, as the projects illustrated in the following pages suggest.   M.M.

The Marika-Alderton House

EASTERN ARNHEM LAND, AUSTRALIA

Glenn Murcutt designed this building to respond to a series of attempts – earlier ones failed – to realize an economic dwelling prototype where Australian Aborigines could live. The earlier solutions proposed did not respect the rules of local architecture, which need to confront a very hot and humid climate, and they were by no means comfortable; for these reasons they were quickly abandoned or destroyed by their intended users. Murcutt, helped by his first commissioner, an Aboriginal artist, decided to resolve the problem with a building that would "rest gently upon the land" and would open out toward the surrounding nature, respecting and adapting to its rhythms. The inspiration for the project, a building capable of "opening, closing, and breathing like a plant," came from nature itself.

The project design arose from the desire to respond to the local climatic conditions by combining certain strategies of passive cooling, such as natural ventilation and shading, to create interior climatic comfort that preceding solutions did not take into consideration. The rooms dedicated to rest are situated in the southwest area of the dwelling (which, in this part of the world, is coolest in the evening) so the inhabitants could sleep comfortably, while the spaces used primarily in the morning, such as the kitchen, the washroom, and the sitting room, occupy the opposite corner of the house.

Natural ventilation was obtained by renouncing, first of all, window panes, a choice that also s the economy of the reduces the cost of construction. Living spaces remain primarily open to the outdoors, allowing abundant air to enter into the interior, where it can circulate freely and finally be expelled by means of a series of chimneys strategically

arranged on the cover. Interior ventilation benefits from the design of the cover and the interior walls, which close before meeting with the ceiling. The air also circulates freely beneath the dwelling, which is raised from the earth to preserve it, also, from the frequent squalls that occur throughout the year. Shading elements include a combination of sizable overhangs on the cover, adjustable curtains, and a series of window shutters that form the exterior walls of the house and can be opened or closed as needed, allowing easy adaptation to the variable weather of the area. The shutters were analyzed – along with the absence of windowpanes, the building's steel structure, and

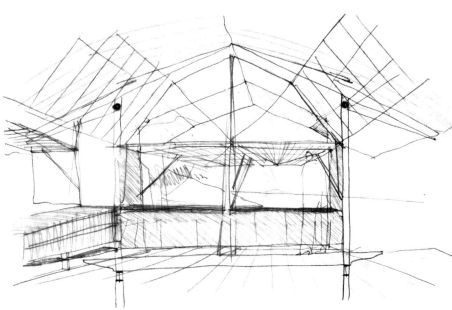

20 top In the Marika-Alderton House, the sheet metal roof protrudes laterally from the building's profile, ensuring shade on the longer sides and keeping the interior spaces from overheating.

20-21 The shell opens toward the exterior by means of a series of movable partitions that allow maximum ventilation of the spaces, responding, at the same time, to the aborigines' need to live immersed in nature.

21 bottom Murcutt's perspective sketch for studying the system of opening toward the exterior for some of the lateral walls without windows, as well as connections between these and the roof.

the profile of the cover – to make sure the building could resist the power of the hurricanes that periodically occur here.

Simple, economical, easily available materials were used for the construction, such as plywood for the walls, sawed wood for the walls and window shutters, steel for the bearing frame, and undulated sheet metal for the cover. This choice – combined with certain project planning precautions, such as centralized arrangements for installations – allowed the use of prefabricated materials, thereby keeping construction costs to a minimum. The entire structure was assembled in just two days, without using particularly specialized labor.   B.S.

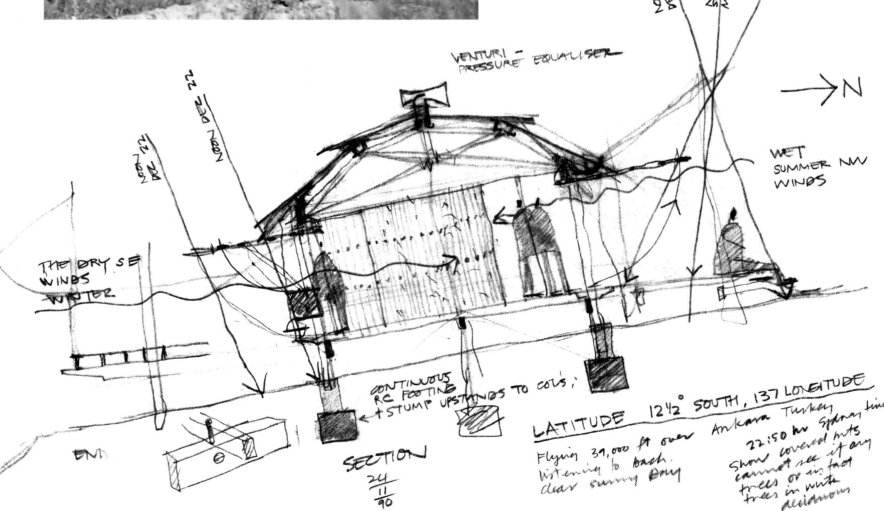

22 top The building is raised from the ground to protect it from the frequent sea storms that occur throughout the year.

22 bottom and 23 The sketches show how the project was completed by a careful bioclimatic study, allowing the building to be profiled as a function of sun inclination and wind direction.

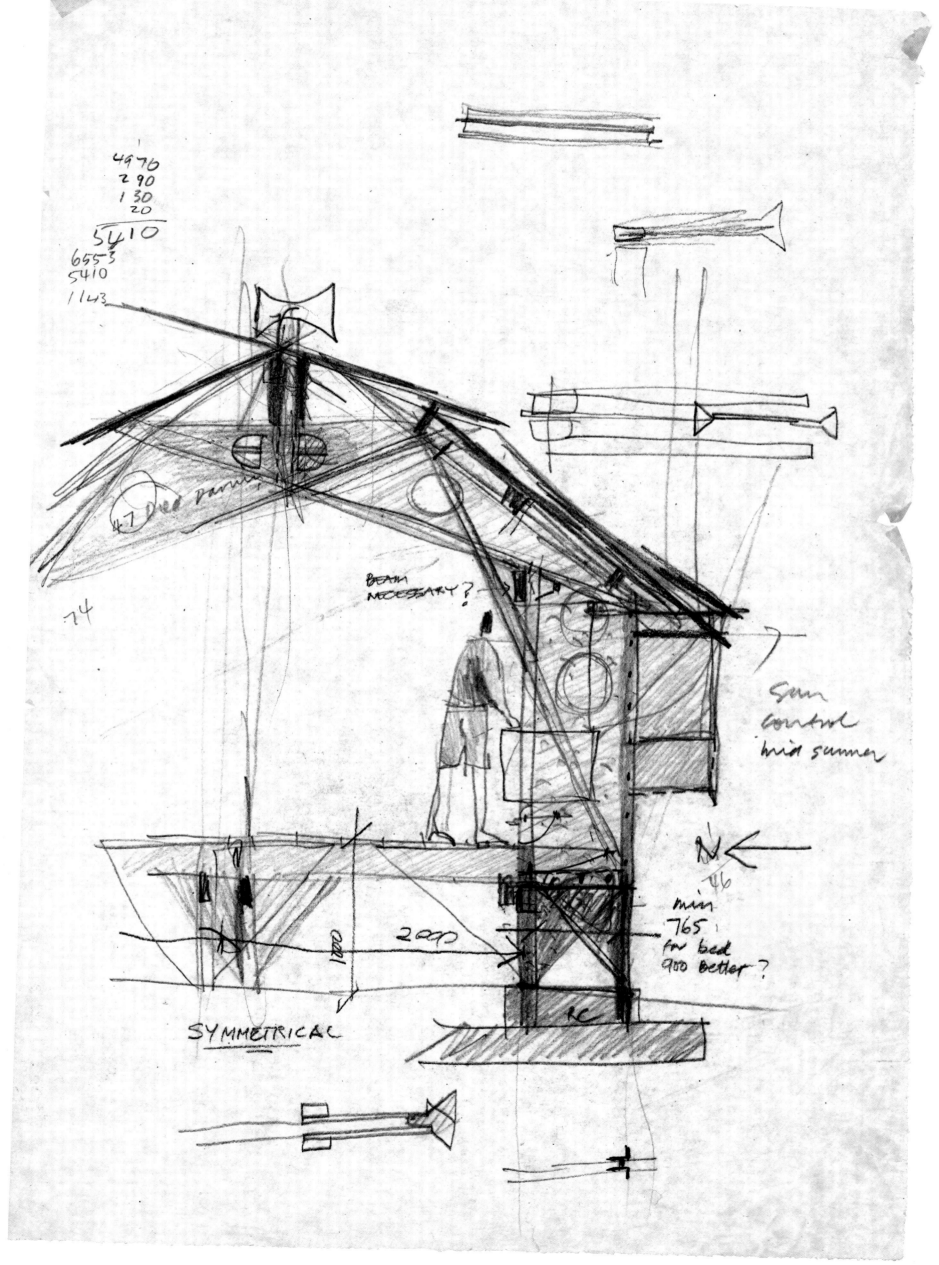

4970
290
130
20
5410
6553
5410
1143

74

47 bed room

BEAM
NECESSARY?

Sun
control
mid summer

min
765
for bed
900 better?

2000

SYMMETRICAL

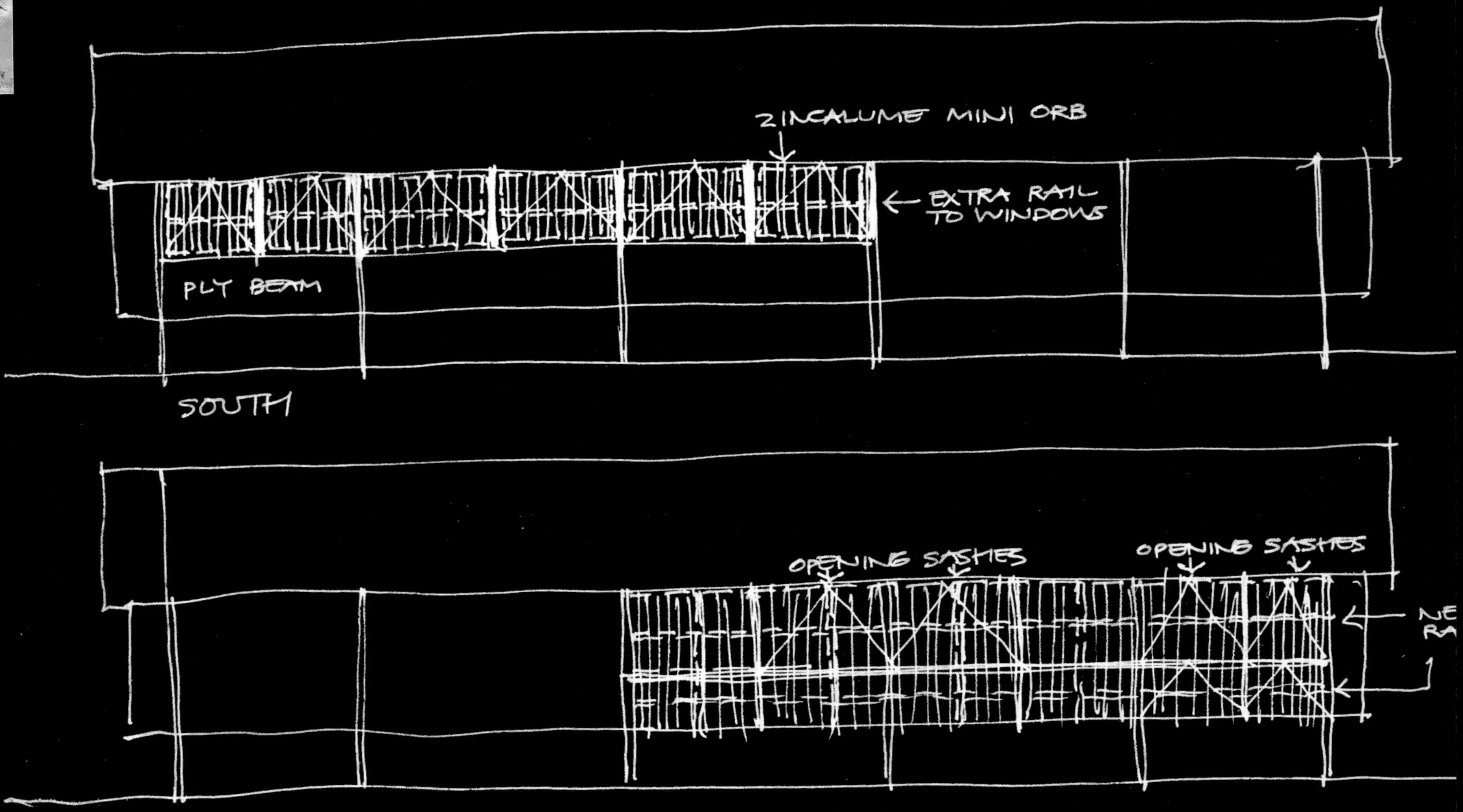

GLENN MURCUTT

ZINCALUME MINI ORB

← EXTRA RAIL TO WINDOWS

PLY BEAM

SOUTH

OPENING SASHES   OPENING SASHES

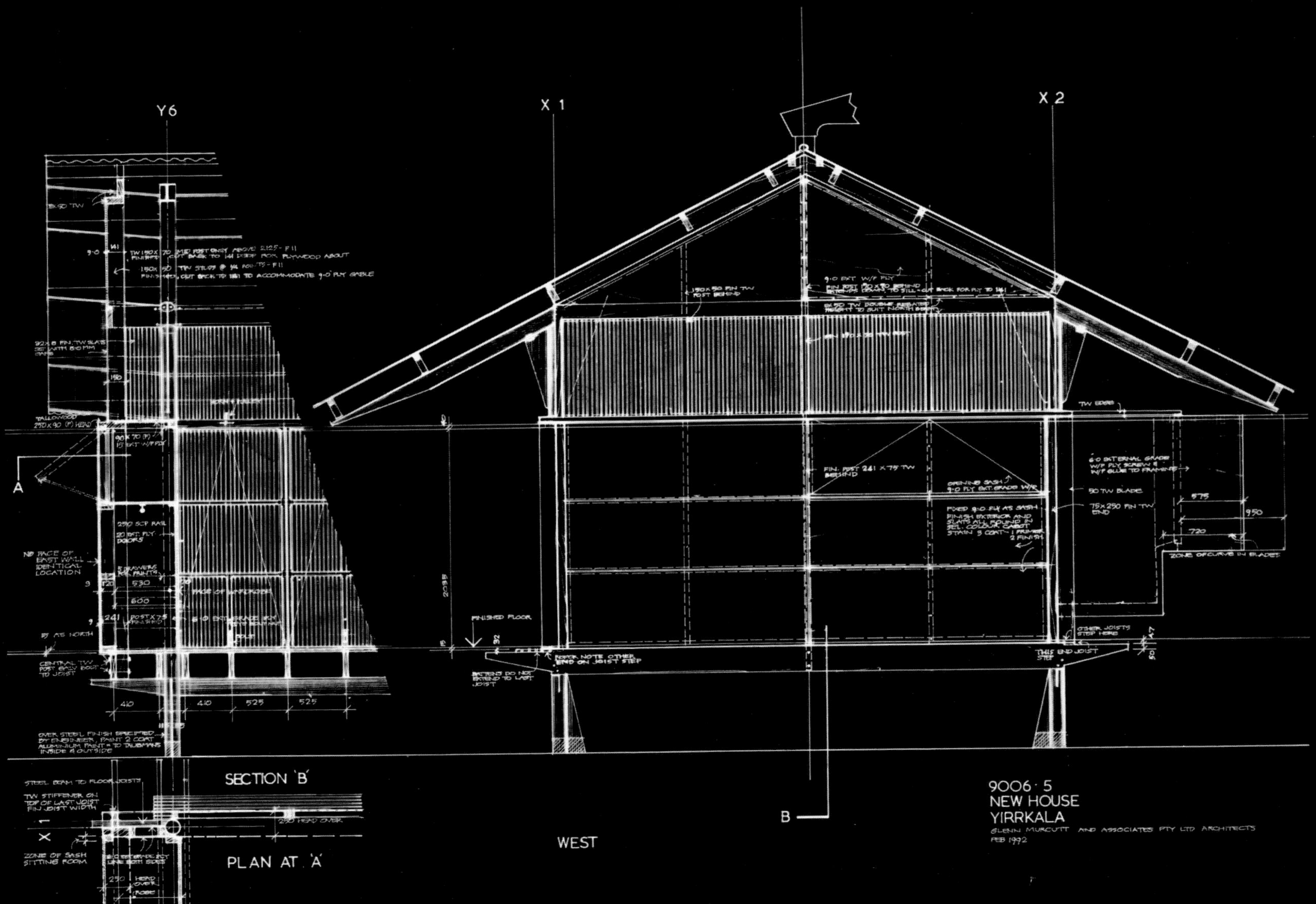

NE

Y6   X1   X2

A

SECTION 'B'

B

WEST

PLAN AT 'A'

9006 · 5
NEW HOUSE
YIRRKALA
GLENN MURCUTT AND ASSOCIATES PTY LTD ARCHITECTS
FEB 1992

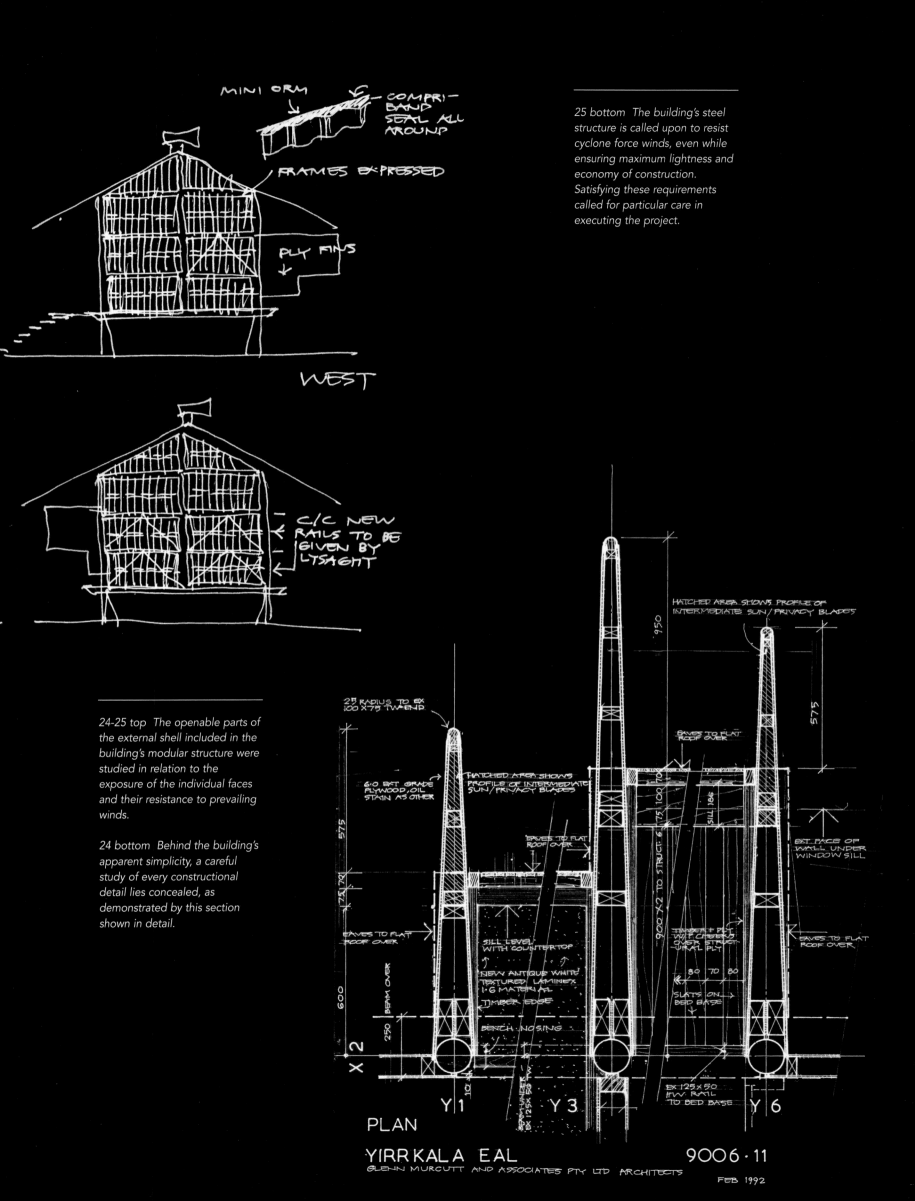

MINI ORM

COMPRI-BAND SEAL ALL AROUND

FRAMES EXPRESSED

PLY FINS

WEST

C/C NEW RAILS TO BE GIVEN BY LTSAGHT

25 *bottom The building's steel structure is called upon to resist cyclone force winds, even while ensuring maximum lightness and economy of construction. Satisfying these requirements called for particular care in executing the project.*

24-25 *top The openable parts of the external shell included in the building's modular structure were studied in relation to the exposure of the individual faces and their resistance to prevailing winds.*

24 *bottom Behind the building's apparent simplicity, a careful study of every constructional detail lies concealed, as demonstrated by this section shown in detail.*

HATCHED AREA SHOWS PROFILE OF INTERMEDIATE SUN/PRIVACY BLADES

950

575

25 RADIUS TO EX 100 X 75 TW END

6·0 EXT GRADE PLYWOOD, OIL STAIN AS OTHER

HATCHED AREA SHOWS PROFILE OF INTERMEDIATE SUN/PRIVACY BLADES

575

EAVES TO FLAT ROOF OVER

EAVES TO FLAT ROOF OVER

75/70

SILL LEVEL WITH COUNTERTOP

NEW ANTIQUE WHITE TEXTURED LAMINEX 1·6 MATERIAL

TIMBER EDGE

600

BENCH NOSING

250 BEAM OVER

EAVES TO FLAT ROOF OVER

TIMBER + PLY W/F CHEEKS OVER STRUCTURAL PLY

80 70 80

SLATS ON BED BASE

EXT FACE OF WALL UNDER WINDOW SILL

EAVES TO FLAT ROOF OVER

EX 125 X 50 H.W. RAIL TO BED BASE

X 2

Y 1

Y 3

Y 6

PLAN

YIRRKALA EAL

9006·11

GLENN MURCUTT AND ASSOCIATES PTY LTD ARCHITECTS

FEB 1992

Residência na Barra do Sahy

SÃO SEBASTIÃO, BRAZIL

ntroduced into an ecosystem of great importance, but also among the most threatened, the vacation home at Barra do Sahy – a beach along the north coast of the state of São Paulo – was conceived with the intention of minimizing modifications to the environment and, instead, of facilitating contact with it.

The environmental and climatic characteristics of the place are not conditions to be opposed, but rather opportunities to be exploited using intelligence.

In this zone of the Mata Atlântica, a rainforest along the Atlantic coast of Brazil, the humidity reaches 100 percent and the heat is constant throughout the year. With these conditions, the relationship between a dwelling's exterior and its interior is especially important.

Erected on a platform of reinforced cement and rising from the soil in order not to permanently weaken the sandy ground, the house is composed of a series of adjacent spaces, separated from one another by walls of cement blocks. There are no corridors connecting the three bedrooms/bathrooms within the ample day area: access is always from the outside. The living space spreads out, underscored by the use of quartzite flooring, not only for the interior spaces but also for the exterior spaces of the basement. The almost complete opening of the façades further accents this effect of total interpenetration between interior and exterior.

The whole is covered by a ventilated roof, consisting of a mantle fashioned from a double layer of aluminum sheet metal with interposed insulation, supported by a light prefabricated structure made of *jatobá* wood, particularly compact and suitable for such use, even on the outside.

For the wooden structure, the two young planners from São

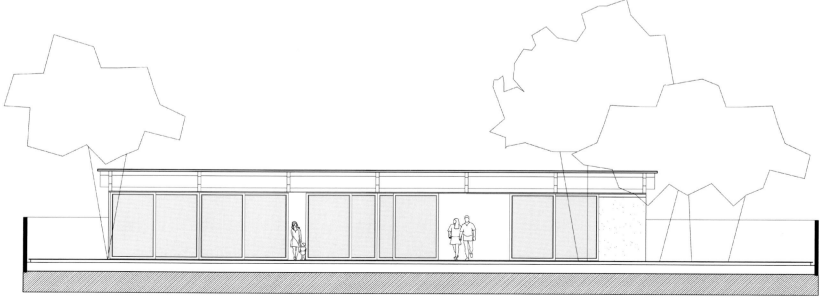

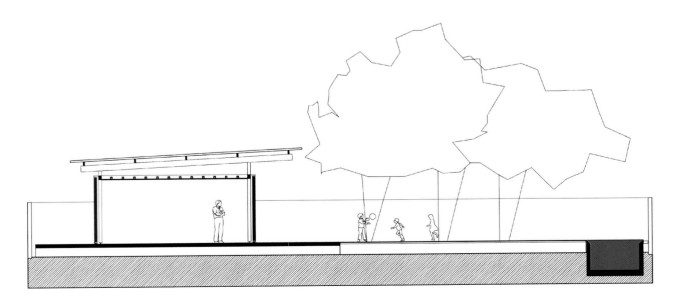

26 bottom Six spans of 3.85 m each (about 12.6 ft) define the geometry of the façade, which can be opened entirely except for the half module of the bathroom/laundry.

26-27 The large sliding glass walls eliminate all barriers between interior and exterior, revealing the lightness of the wooden structure.

27 bottom The roof can be raised toward the beach to access of invite marine breezes.

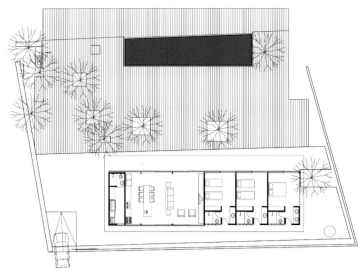

NITSCHE ARQUITETOS ASSOCIADOS

Paulo turned to ITA Construtora, the company headed by structural engineer Hélio Olga de Souza Jr., who is involved in many of the most interesting architectural works realized in wood in recent years in Brazil. It is often not considered relevant to cite the construction company in a project description, but the contribution by ITA Construtora to this, as to other buildings, is also closely connected to important environmental aspects, such as obtaining wood from forests managed in a sustainable manner and taking care to optimize the size of components so as to minimize debris.

Among the environmentally friendly strategies implemented in the building, besides the ventilated cover, is a capacious reservoir at the north corner of the platform for recovery of rainwater. M.M.

28 top The lot has a surface of barely 800 sq m (about 8600 sq ft) and the house is built close to the boundary wall to the north. At the opposite end in the garden is the swimming pool, narrow and elongated in form. The rainwater collection reservoir is in the corner opposite the vehicle entry.

28 bottom A wooden floor, of local origin and deriving from certified sustainable forest, defines an open area living room space nearby the swimming pool.

28-29 and 29 top The kitchen (upper photo), dining room, and living room (center photo) are grouped into one large single space, the focal point of life in this vacation home, built for a family that usually resides in the city of São Paulo.

30-31 top The entrance to the dwelling, quite discreet, is located on the east side, composed of a simple door intentionally camouflaged within the building's wooden covering.

30-31 bottom The east prospect of the building faces the access road to the lot, with a limited number of openings so as to preserve the occupants' privacy.

Villa Lena

ESPOO, FINLAND

Koponen designed this villa, in which he himself lives, with the intention of developing the theme of the "single space," a concept translated into practice by means of a shell ensuring a visual continuum between interior and exterior, and through the design of interiors organized as a succession of uninterrupted spaces. The driving idea for the project was to permit nature – the building is immersed in woods of birch and fir, a typical Finnish landscape – to enter through the completely transparent walls of the daytime zone with its western exposure. The other sides remain largely closed, not only to ensure privacy from neighbors and street activity, but also to limit heat loss. On the north and south sides, two small transparent patios have been fashioned, facing toward the interior of the building and functioning as wells of natural light for the spaces farthest down. Inside the house, the various living functions intercross in a fluid space, defined only by furniture and light draperies, except for the service blocks containing bathrooms and kitchen in special boxlike structures. The entire structure is built of wood, a natural material recalling the surrounding forest, for the ideal realization of a further form of continuum. The shell and the sparse interior walls were erected using a structure composed of a bearing frame insulated internally with mineral wool, covered with rigid wooden panels, with a layer of external ventilation fashioned under the external plank work, of larch wood, optimizing the thermal conditions of the wall

31 bottom A good part of the building is suspended above ground by a bearing system of posts, chosen to respect the natural slope of the terrain.

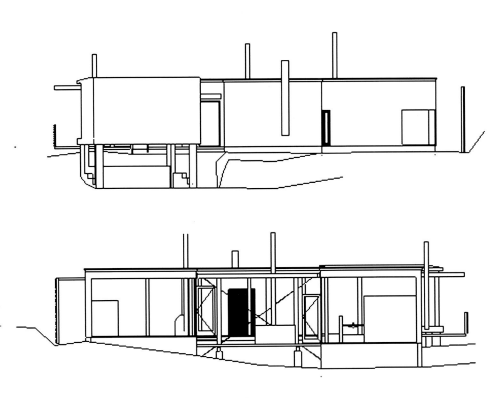

packet. The floor, concrete with blue and clear crushed glass mixed in, is thickly insulated. The whole was realized using a series of prefabricated elements, dry mounted on-site, thus optimizing the use of time and materials; many of the coverings were realized on-site by the architect himself. A carpenter in his youth, he is well acquainted with the secrets of wood. In correspondence with the large windows, the bearing function is performed by simple red fir posts, allowing free lighting and therefore maximum transparency for the glass-paneled shell. The shell, with no visible frame other than for the few parts that can be opened, was created with large slabs of IGU (insulating glass unit) with reduced-emission coating, filled with argon gas. Air exchange is provided by a mechanical ventilating system that recovers heat from the exhaust air, further reducing the thermal requirement for heating the entire house, and heating the spaces partly with the heated air.   B.S.

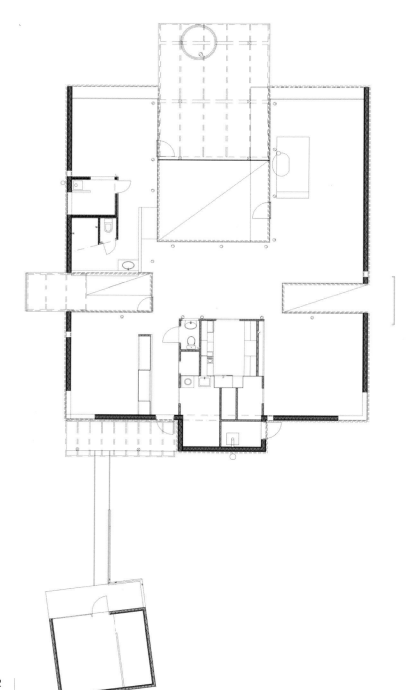

32 The plan of the building reveals a fluid sequence of interior spaces, in which each respective function is assigned only by virtue of the furnishings present.

32-33 The focal point of the dwelling is the central courtyard, onto which the majority of the interior spaces face, through a continuous, transparent shell, allowing communication – and visibility between the various zones of the house.

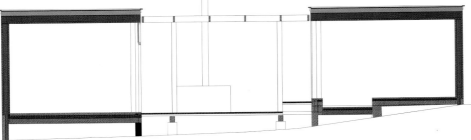

*33 bottom The transverse
section shows the downward
incline of the terrain upon which
the building rests, with the base
structured to adapt to the slope.*

Villa Lena

34 The central courtyard was conceived as an open-air living room, completely immersed in the surrounding woods of birch and red fir.

35 The space reserved for the study is located in an independent structure, completely closed on the street side. On the opposite side, it connects to the living quarters by means of an exterior wooden walkway.

36-37 The inner courtyard is structured on various levels to respect the slope of the terrain and, at the same time, to realize a particular spatial situation, enhanced by various sculptural works.

38-39 The clefts on the north and south sides of the building are interpreted as wells of light, illuminating the rooms situated farthest down. One of the two was conceived as a Zen garden, characterized by shards of blue glass.

39 Inside the dwelling, as well, one perceives the sensation of living immersed in nature, by virtue of the large glass windows installed all around.

House of steel and wood

RANÓN, SPAIN

Ecosistema Urbano is a Madrid-based studio strongly committed to themes of sustainability, particularly as regards planning and management of public spaces. In defining the principles inspiring their work, the planning team makes recourse to terms starting with the letter R, as in the famous "4 Rs" (Reduce, Reuse, Recycle, Repair). These are posited as the basis of an attitude of consciousness of today's environmental and social challenges. At the house of steel and wood at Rañon in the Asturias, other *Rs* for "Revision" and "Reversibility" are especially highlighted.

One can note a contemporary revision of certain archetypes of the vernacular architecture of the Asturias: the elevated granary, the glass-paneled bow window, and the use of wood for the structure and shell. The modern interpretation thus provides a combination and reinterpretation of formal and constructional typologies from the local architecture. As always,

attention to that which already exists, materially or as cultural heritage, takes priority in the elaborate process of the Ecosistema Urbano architects.

The building adapts to the climatic conditions and respects the trees growing in this wooded area. The house minimizes its impact on the terrain and on the landscape as it rises from the ground, resting upon just four points. The original slope of the terrain is maintained, and the grassy mantle spreads under the house.

This structure made of steel and wood embodies the concept of reversibility in architecture: it can be completely dismantled. The modification of the environmental context, always associated with the construction of a building, aims to favor the possibility of resetting the starting conditions. It does not intend to establish itself as a permanent mark.

The shell mixes Douglas fir and forest pine in planks of

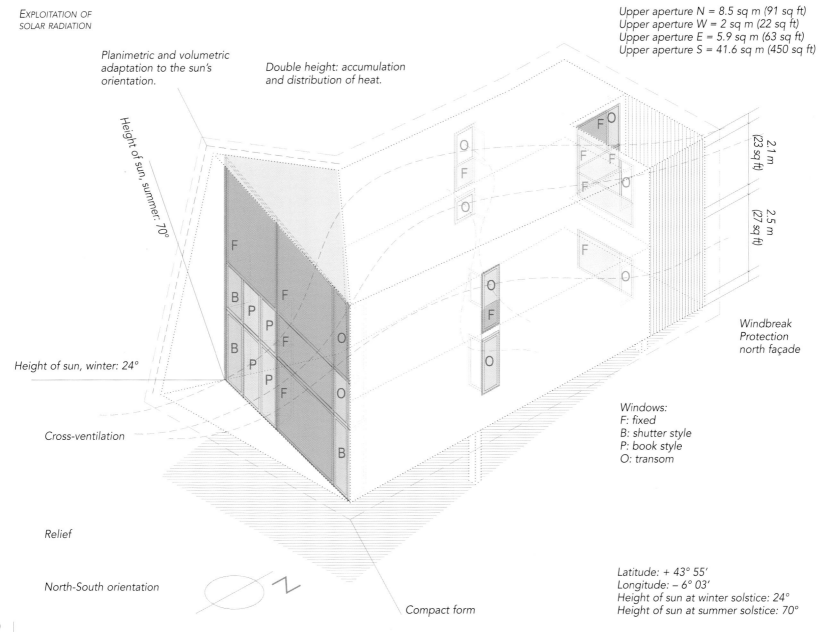

EXPLOITATION OF SOLAR RADIATION

Planimetric and volumetric adaptation to the sun's orientation.

Double height: accumulation and distribution of heat.

Upper aperture N = 8.5 sq m (91 sq ft)
Upper aperture W = 2 sq m (22 sq ft)
Upper aperture E = 5.9 sq m (63 sq ft)
Upper aperture S = 41.6 sq m (450 sq ft)

Height of sun, summer: 70°

2.1 m (23 sq ft)

2.5 m (27 sq ft)

Height of sun, winter: 24°

Windbreak Protection north façade

Cross-ventilation

Windows:
F: fixed
B: shutter style
P: book style
O: transom

Relief

North-South orientation

Compact form

Latitude: + 43° 55'
Longitude: – 6° 03'
Height of sun at winter solstice: 24°
Height of sun at summer solstice: 70°

40 The building was conceived on the basis of a careful examination of the relationship with the local climate: the morphology of the terrain and the orientation and direction of the principal winds and air currents dictated the architect's bioclimatic strategy .

41 By contrast with the other façades, the south side is completely paneled with glass so as to obtain the best passive solar gain. The glass paneling defines a double-height space that functions as a heat accumulation zone. In the milder seasons the parts of the façade that can be opened ensure cross ventilation.

41 bottom The bearing structure is realized entirely in steel and then enclosed by a double shell of wood with a thick layer of insulation.

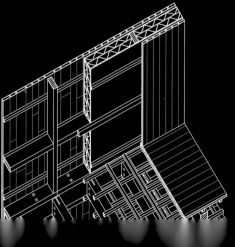

42 top and 43 top left The entire house is raised off the ground; the grassy mantle and vegetation present on the lot are left intact. If the building is dismantled, it will leave but few traces on the ground.

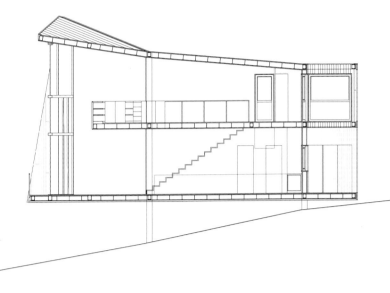

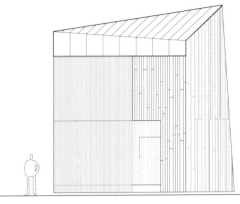

varying widths, a combination of elements that integrates the house into the landscape as though forming the bark of a new type of tree. This is a house that fuses with nature, without the use of heating or air-conditioning systems: through its orientation and geometry the building adapts to the local clime.

The two-story space, entirely of glass, faces south; adjustable wood fillets are used for screening from the sun, allowing hygrothermal regulation to best manage the interior microclimate.

The longer façades are almost totally blind so as to minimize heat dispersion. All spaces in the house have the possibility of cross-ventilation.

The two-story plan is not simply a compositional or spatial choice. It is a fundamental bio-climatic apparatus, the pivotal point for regulating the temperature. Compact space, optimizing the form factor. Functional flexibility in a dwelling that can be transformed and subdivided in time.   M.M.

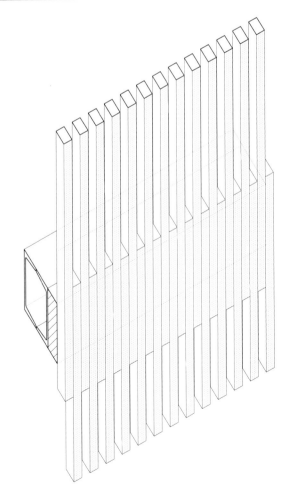

42-43 By contrast with provisions for the south façade, the other perimeter walls have only a few openings in order to minimize heat loss.

43 top right, center and bottom The side facing north is characterized by a screening of wooden fillets for the small open area leading to the entrance.

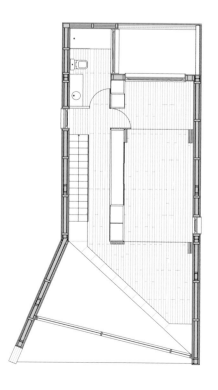
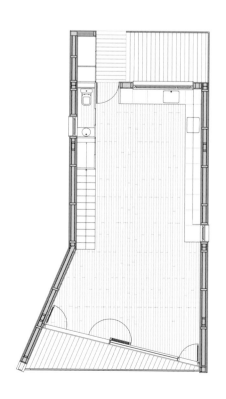
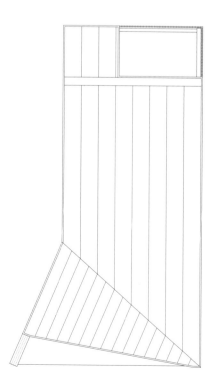

44-45 The night zone is a large, single space facing onto the double volume corresponding to the south façade and toward the north entry; the double exposure ensures natural ventilation during the hottest season.

44 bottom The layout of the interior provides two ample open spaces. On the entry level are the kitchen zone, dining area, and living room, united into one single space. On the upper level, another single space hosts the bedroom.

45 bottom The two floors are connected internally by a wooden staircase rising parallel to the west side of the building. The interior, covered totally with wood, transmits a sensation of warmth, contributing to the psycho-physical well-being of the inhabitants.

46-47 top The curvilinear form of the building follows the contours of the road. The complex is composed of two volumes of three floors each, separated by a cleft between the two units where the entryway is located.

46-47 bottom The design of the north and west façades demonstrates the desire of the commissioners and project planners to maintain the height of the new living complex at the average level of the surrounding buildings, even while highlighting the intervention with contemporary features and materials.

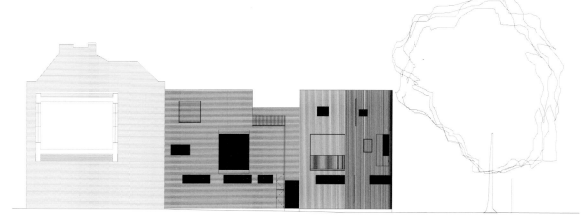

Carmarthen Place
LONDON, UNITED KINGDOM

This reconstruction, situated in the London neighborhood of Southbank, involves a lot previously destined for a speculative residential project to which the local residents were firmly opposed. Envisioning a complex more consonant with the context of neighboring 17th-century row houses, they acquired the site in order to preserve the peculiar qualities of this urban space. Their commissioned artist and architect, in collaboration with the AIR design studio, thus became construction entrepreneurs, realizing a building composed of a studio outfitted with an exterior courtyard and two dwelling units. The dimensions of the building were determined, above all, by the economic value of the dwellings, which were destined to be sold to cover the cost of the entire project.

The results of the enterprise exceeded expectations: the apartments, completed in 2006, were successfully sold, and the building was honored with a Wood Award the following year.

The building's massive prefabricated system in wood proved advantageous not only for the small work site, but also for economy of construction. The structure was brought to completion in just 12 days and is highly energy-efficient. The exterior was covered with fillets of Siberian larch; the internal coverings were reduced to a minimum in order to maintain the advantages afforded by the solid wood in terms of hygroscopic properties and soundness. Ceilings and walls display the decoratively exposed fir structure, while the floors are covered, for contrast, in clear resin. The building sports an extensive green roof to cool the rooms on the top floor in summer and, at the same time, reduce the risk of flooding from heavy rains.

The constructional system was also selected based on in-depth iconographic research by the commissioners/designers regarding the history of this part of the city, where wood was often used for construction in the past. The new complex harmonizes with the pre-existing architecture. Its two sections are separated by a space marking the entrance to the courtyard derived from the back. The first, an artist's studio, is a two-story building, closed to the street and sloping downward toward the courtyard, onto which it faces with a curvilinear,

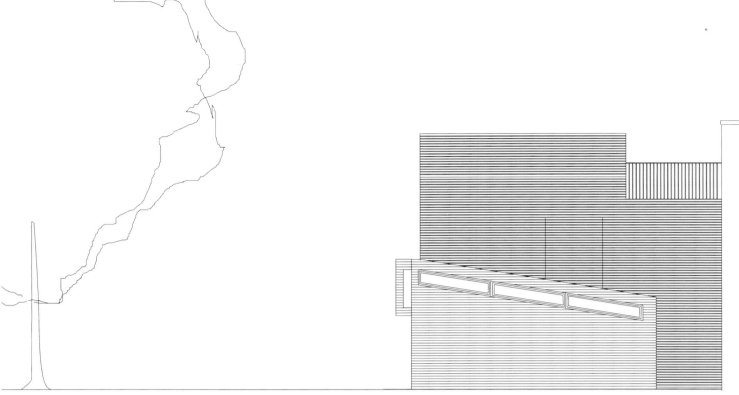

glass-paneled profile designed to make best use of natural light. The open space is connected to the 17th-century dwelling at the back by means of a glass door and an external brickwork stairway. The second section of Carmarthen Place contains two apartments distributed over three floors, separated by a narrow corridor for distribution of the entryways. Each apartment was planned with bedrooms and bathrooms on the ground floor, the kitchen and dining area on the first level, and, on the top floor, the living room and study corner facing onto a terrace. This particular allotment of spaces was conceived to make the most of the available natural light without compromising the privacy of the inhabitants – a choice that is also evident in the distribution of the openings on the side of the building facing the street. B.S.

48 top The complex also includes a low structure where the owners' studio is located, with the possibility of access to the interior courtyard onto which it faces through a broad wall of glass.

49 top Both of the dwelling units host living rooms on the upper

level, so as to best exploit natural lighting and ensure a view of the city's rooftops.

48-49 The studio borders in the back with the owner's residence, sharing its inner courtyard, where a connecting stairway has been created between the two units.

50 top The entire structure of the building, including the interior stairways, was realized using a prefabricated system composed of monolithic laminated wood walls.

50 bottom A space for a studio has even been fashioned on the top floor, quite luminous owing to the natural light streaming in from the street and the inner courtyard.

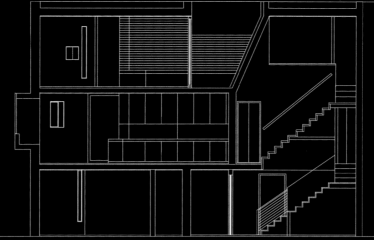

50-51 *On the intermediate level of each dwelling unit are the kitchen and dining area, illuminated primarily by means of natural light coming through a skylight in the ceiling.*

51 top *Each dwelling unit extends over three floors. On the lowest level, besides the entryway, are the bedrooms and bathrooms, which require less natural light.*

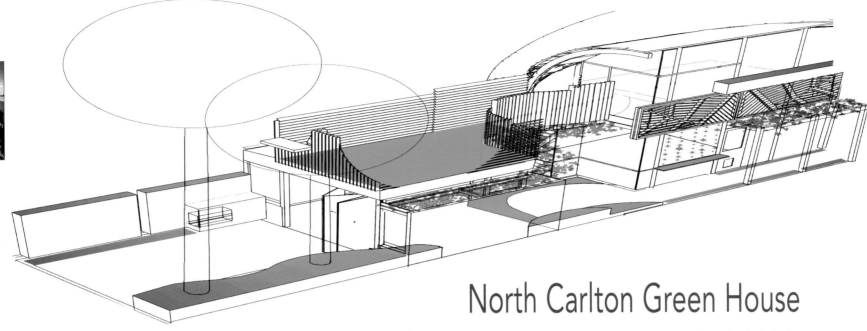

North Carlton Green House

MELBOURNE, AUSTRALIA

The owners of the small building in a row of Victorian style residences, built on a lot of just 166 sq m (about 1790 sq ft), expressed the need to increase the space available to them, both for dwelling and garden. They requested particular attention from the architects toward reducing to a minimum the to keep consumption of energy and resources to a minimum.

The architects succeeded with this difficult task by taking inspiration from the commissioners' passion for gardening, which suggested a continuing relationship between nature and the inhabited space, achieved by alternating the new rooms with closed or open green spaces, capable of bringing the natural elements, including water, to the interior of the dwelling. Diffuse natural light and plants make the interior spaces more healthful and, at the same time, more pleasant to live in.

The project developed despite numerous constraints, connected not only with the nature of the space but also with the historical value of the protected building which, in part, is protected. But this did not prevent the project planners from expanding the living space from 90 to 132 sq m (from about 970 sq ft to about 1420 sq ft), and the garden, from 20 to 35 sq m (from about 215 sq ft to about 380 sq ft).

The curved section of the new roof, fashioned on the first story, recalls the profile of the palms found on site and, at the same time, allows them to avoid shading the adjacent properties, and to conceal the upper floor from the row of Victorian style buildings composing the protected context

52 top The axonometric view shows how the majority of the north face of the building is composed of transparent walls to let in sunlight and heat even on the coldest days of the year.

52 bottom The majority of the first floor is occupied by a hanging garden, responding to the clients' requirement to expand the green surface area in spite of the diminutive dimensions of the lot.

53 The north face takes on the appearance of a greenhouse, which allows the owners to pursue their gardening passion even while indoors.

54 The space containing the kitchen and dining area faces onto the interior courtyard. A sliding mechanism allows the transparent wall between the two to open completely. The kitchen-dining room's other two walls are also of glass, ensuring maximum luminosity for the space.

55 The ground-floor living room is especially luminous owing to its glass walls and its double height. A portion of the space is occupied by a mezzanine hosting the studio on the upper floor.

on the street. The flat cover over the kitchen and dining corner, corresponding to a single level in the building, constituted byconsists of a green roof that contributes to the thermal insulation of the interior. Part of the house rises two floors and opens toward the north, allowing sunlight and heat to penetrate into every room of the building. This is achieved in part withsome bricks recovered from the pre-existing building and with floors of reinforced cement. These latter are heated using a radiant installation, powered by solar panels arranged on the roof.

The materials employed for the construction provide a remarkable useful thermal mass, both to optimize the passive heat produced inside the dwelling on the coldest days of the year, and also to maintain the interior temperature at comfortable levels even on the hottest days. The strategy for passive cooling is completed by the presence of deciduous plants and of louvered fixtures which provide optimum shading and natural ventilation. The latter is facilitated by the buildings' profile, specifically designed toward this purpose to exploit the chimney effect and to expel hot air through the upper floor on the hottest days.

The building is equipped with an efficient system for recovery of rainwater, used for laundry; the gray water resulting from this activity is used to irrigate the numerous plants cultivated both outside and inside the dwelling, by means of a drip-system installation, optimizing use of the water itself.   B.S.

56 top The master bathroom on the lower floor opens toward the exterior through a French door facing onto an alleyway in the garden, which also allows light into one of the bedrooms.

56 bottom The planimetry reveals a continuous alternation of interior and exterior spaces on both levels, conceived to allow

the correct bioclimatic orientation for the building in spite of the original arrangement and elongated form of the lot.

57 The study, equipped with a bathroom, is the only room on the upper floor. Its curvilinear roof is designed to conceal the extra floor with respect to the profile of the buildings along the street.

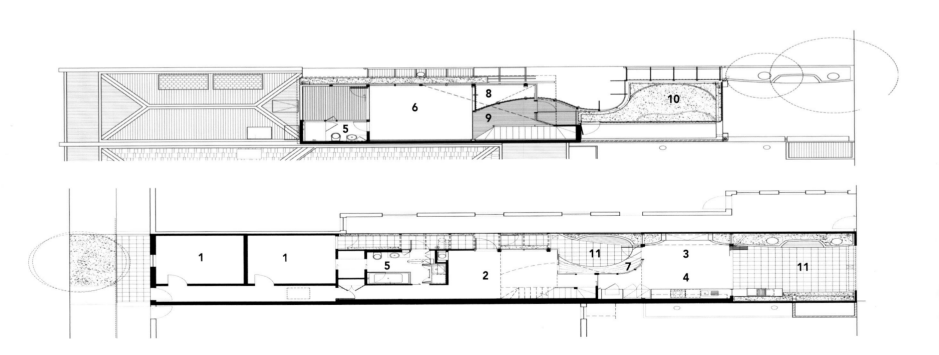

LEGEND

1 bed	**5** bath room	**9** bridge
2 living	**6** studio	**10** roof garden
3 dining	**7** pond	**11** courtyard
4 kitchen	**8** void	

58 bottom left Constructed on a terrain occupied by a still-active coconut palm plantation, the Palmyra House, seen from the beach, appears immersed in the vegetation.

Palmyra House

NANDGAON, INDIA

Bijoy Jain and his Mumbai Studio just received a special mention at the 12th Venice Architecture Biennale. Invited to exhibit their works in the spaces of the Arsenal, the project planners set up a sort of temporary headquarters for their studio. Rather than highlighting previous projects and realizations, they wanted to accentuate their methodology, -- rather than previous projects and realizations -- involving which involves very close connections between conception and construction, and between project planner, artisan, and craftsmen. The studio-laboratory is the space where different experiences and forms of knowledge coalesce, with the and relationships develop as building proceeds on the construction site. It is a vision that exalts the collective character of architecture, light-years away from the media system of the star architect.

It is only by knowing the extraordinary character of this group, which Bijoy Jain defines as "a human infrastructure of architects and expert artisans who directly design and build their projects," that one can fully grasp the merit of an architectural work that is already fascinating in and of itself, such as that of the Palmyra House. Partially concealed among the coconut palms of a still active plantation, this house-refuge opens toward the west, toward the beach, along the shore south of Mumbai, on the Arabian Sea, in the state of Maharashtra.

The dwelling is organized wo constructed bodies into two sections separated from one another by the irregularly shaped open space hosting the expanse of a long basin of water, which is both swimming pool and regulating element for the microclimate.

The distribution of the spaces is extremely fluid, as is the constant relationship with the exterior. The upper floors host the bedrooms, bathrooms and sitting areas. On the ground floor are more sitting areas, a kitchen, a large dining room, sanitary facilities, and a bedroom.

The two volumes are realized in wood: hard local wood for the structures and equally resistant wood taken directly on-site from palm trees of the variety *Borassus flabellifer* (palmyra palm) for the closing elements, with which the two sections are entirely coated. The transparency and lightness the two structures take

58-59 A long swimming pool separates the two structures, defining a space out in the open that becomes the focal point of the composition, but also an important element for regulation of the microclimate.

59 top right The shell of the two buildings is totally open to marine breezes. The apparently closed walls are, in reality, composed of panels of thin wooden fillets to ensure optimal ventilation of the interiors as well as protection from the intense rays of the sun.

on seem inspired by the way coconut palm fronds screen the sun, allowing just enough radiation to penetrate to create a suffused shadow, into which blades of light penetrate, animating the space.

The façades are covered by a system of fixed panels that can be opened, screening the light to avoid overheating while allowing the sea breezes to pass through. Only on the north side are the ample glass panels situated in the upper part of the volume left without screening, allowing an adequate influx of natural light. The ventilation system is absolutely natural.

The only parts in masonry are the kitchen, bathrooms, and stairwells, where the stairs are realized in wood with refined carpentry techniques. Copper is used for coating internally and externally; the shower "box" juts out from the first floor, uncovered, as is customary at these latitudes.

The swimming pool is inserted into a complex system of artesian wells that act as conductors to transport the water already available on-site.

Palmyra House is a work of architecture literally "made by hand." In 2010 it received the Aga Khan Architecture Award for placed on its appreciation of local resources and for the artisans' ability to work the traditional materials, projecting them into fully contemporary language.   M.M.

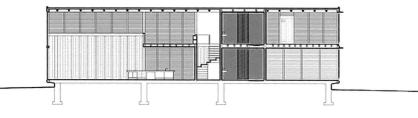

60-61 Even in the project model, the light wooden framework took a definite form quite close to the final result.

60 bottom Inside the two structures, in the portions facing the beach, ample open spaces alternate with subdivided areas.

61 bottom *The sketch of the external shell of one of the two buildings is extraordinary close in appearance to the finished work, showing the texture of the wooden fillets that cover the structure, alternating with a few large empty spaces.*

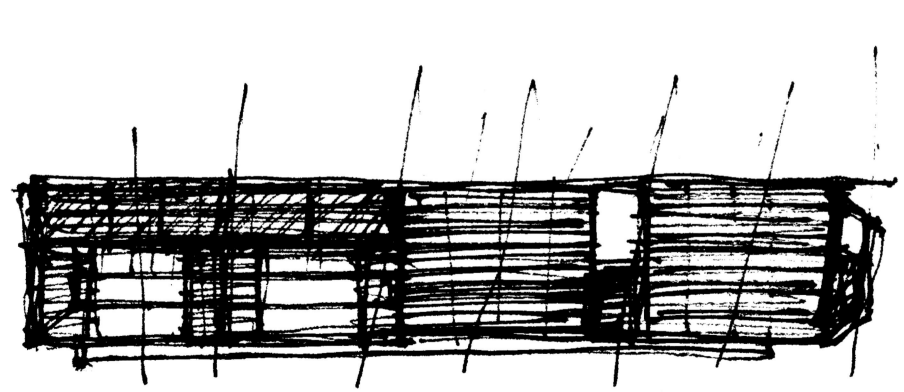

62 top Because this is truly a "handmade" architectural work, its details reveal the skills of the craftsmen.

62 bottom Studio Mumbai Architects functions as a laboratory in which project designers and craftsmen work side by side. The construction site phase, therefore, is not simply execution but an integral part of the creative process.

62-63 In 2010, Palmyra House received the Aga Khan Architecture Award for its appreciation of artisanal abilities and local materials. Wood combines with copper, stone, and a few rare plastered interior walls to define the repertory of materials utilized.

63 bottom The refinement of the carpentry work results from working in such a manner that project planning and realization are closely integrated.

64 Interior and exterior interpenetrate by means of a series of closures, which, once opened, liberate a major part of the façade.

65 top From the half-light of the palm grove to the blinding light of the beach, environmental conditions required a shell that can not only screen the light but also allow air currents to circulate.

65 bottom Positioning the two structures upon the terrain required taking carefully into account not only the existing vegetation, but also an articulate system of artesian wells, conductors of pre-existing water.

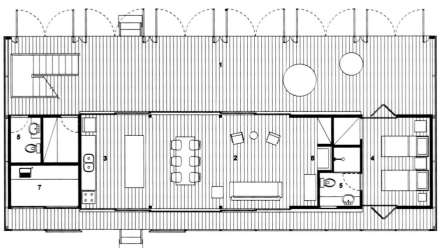

LEGEND

1 porch
2 living/dining area
3 kitchen
4 bedroom
5 bathroom
6 fireplace
7 laundry room

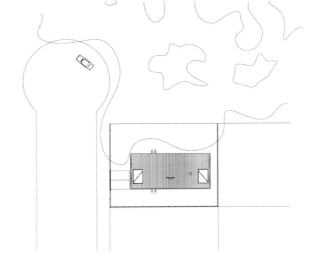

Residência RR

ITAMAMBUCA, BRAZIL

In a country of great contrasts like Brazil, even the theme of sustainable construction can adopt radically different approaches, ranging from the luxury market – well represented in this book by the Casa Folha the present work – to the context of "first necessity" architecture.

Architects Andrade and Morettin work in a sector where the clients' capacity to spend, and their desire to live in a wholesome building respectful of the environment, do not preclude attempts to contain costs.

In realizing this vacation house, the two architects sought to go beyond the specific project theme, attempting to bring into focus a sustainable low-budget house that could be proposed as a model for that vast area of the planet characterized by a humid-tropical climate, with very strong sunlight, equally intense rains, and constantly elevated temperatures.

Constructed a few steps from the beach, the house at Itamambuca is immersed in the luxuriant vegetation of the Atlantic coast of Brazil in the state of São Paulo. To meet the challenges posed by conception took inspiration from the local architectural studio, to determine the mechanisms for adaptation to the environmental conditions, the architects defined a repertory of solutions. These were then reinterpreted and renewed, to give form to what the project planners define as a simple shelter, which seeks to best exploit the characteristics of the warm, humid climate in order to

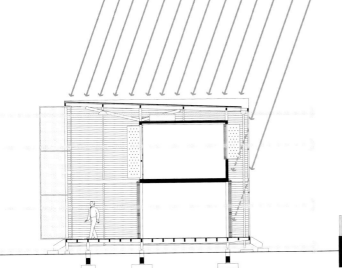

66 bottom The ground floor is organized as one large open space, with only a few spaces sectioned off by walls.

66-67 The narrow façades are almost completely closed, whereas the two wider façades are totally open. The orientation of the building determines the different treatment of the faces of this simple structure.

67 top The small lot from which the building rises is located at the end of a cul-de-sac residential street.

67 bottom The bioclimatic strategy is clear: the house opens allowing cool sea breezes to cross through it, alleviating the constant heat and humidity in this region.

guarantee comfort to the inhabitants without resorting to sophisticated and costly technical installations.

The house's light from the earthshell is raised off the ground, open to breezes but protected from heat and humidity. Going against one of the accepted concepts for sustainable construction in the northern hemisphere, the first principle here was the use of light materials, with reduced thermal inertia and therefore not capable of accumulating heat. The building's structure is of wood, prefabricated so as to minimize production times and, accordingly, the impact on the construction site.

The shell is almost entirely open on the two principal façades, leaving the interior space in contact with the surrounding environment; the only filters are the adjustable panels made of fiberglass and PVC that function as mosquito screens. All the interior spaces benefit from natural ventilation.

The roof and lateral façades are composed of steel cladding with expanded polystyrene insulating filler.

The entire structure is raised 75 cm (about 30 in) off the ground, resting on two reinforced cement columns cast to the purpose. All the other components are prefabricated and can be easily dismantled. The interior partitions are made of OSB panels and plasterboard.

The architectural organism's ability to relate effectively to its environment, with an optimal use of natural lighting and ventilation, allows a great reduction of energy costs, just as the use of prefabricated materials and components reduces construction costs.

Andrade and Morettin are convinced that, with respect to reducing CO_2 emissions, a good project design can do much more than the most sophisticated "green" technologies can.   M.M.

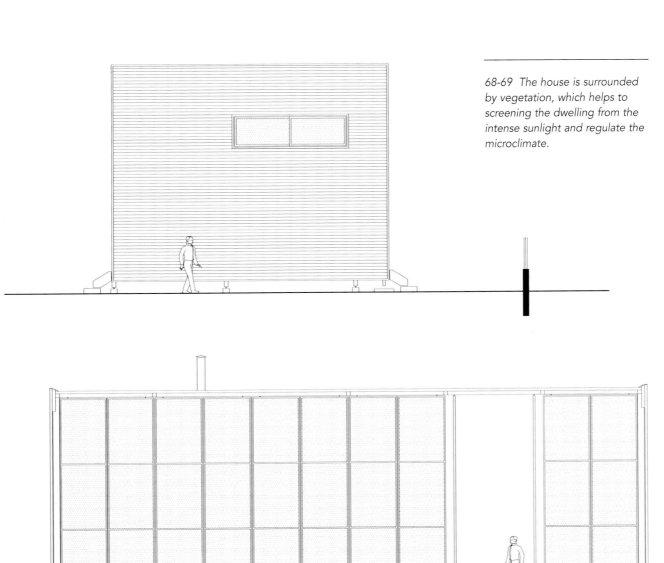

68-69 *The house is surrounded by vegetation, which helps to screening the dwelling from the intense sunlight and regulate the microclimate.*

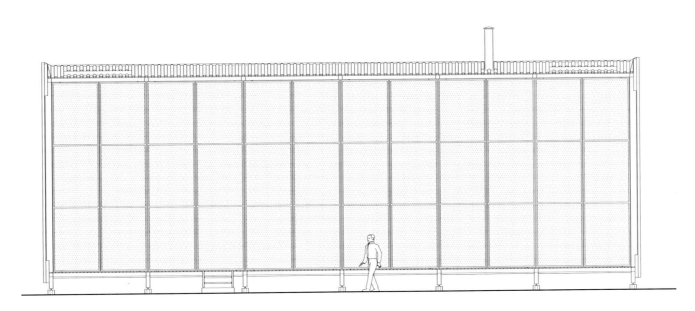

69 top right *On the two shorter façades, the wooden structure is coated in corrugated steel, with limited openings. The volume is raised 75 cm (about 30 in) from the ground.*

69 center right and bottom *The two longer façades are practically identical. Their geometry is defined simply by the partition of the insect screens that cover it entirely.*

70-71 Inside the large volume defined by the external shell, a "home within a home" was realized, better protected from the weather and destined to host more intimate spaces.

71 top The cladding of the two lateral façades with sheet metal contrasts with the absence of a true shell on the longer sides.

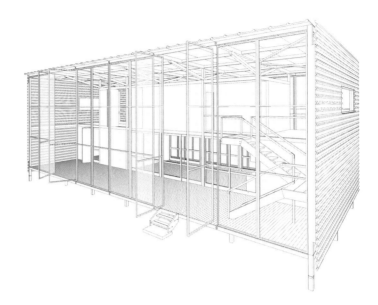

71 bottom The space on the ground floor relates directly to the surrounding landscape and exterior space. The night zone is enclosed, by contrast, within the wooden structure inside the dwelling.

Camouflaged House 3

KARUIZAWA, JAPAN

The inhabitants of this original residence were given the possibility of living in an actual, transparent greenhouse, completely immersed in the woods in the mountainous zone of the prefecture of Nagano. It was one of the projects designed by architect Iguchi in the context of his Fifth World studio, the principal objective of which is to promote diffusion of ecological and sustainable architecture. The habitational model proposed in this project reflects the Shintoist influence in the Japanese people's lifestyle; among the principles of Shinto are respect, veneration, and care of nature, in the sense that, according to this religion, it is from nature that balance of life derives.

The dwelling, which is even called a Greenhouse home, is fully capable of satisfying the desire of someone wishing to live completely surrounded by nature, owing to the complete transparency toward the exterior, obtained by adopting the same constructional solutions utilized for realizing the most modern structures for nursery gardening. The living spaces are distributed into two different sections. The heart of the house is contained in a parallelepiped on one floor whose glass-paneled exterior surfaces are screened by a series of opaque elements, arranged in the interior so as to ensure privacy for the inhabitants. For this reason, the interior of this section receives natural light primarily from above, through a series of transparent elements fashioned on the ceiling.

This part is, for the most part, embedded in the second volume, completely transparent and characterized by a prismatic form in which the principal, inclined face, functioning also as cover, presents a highly elevated slope. This formal choice involves the presence of a space having a very reduced height in correspondence with the lower part of the triangular section, something to which it is generally very difficult to give a solution in functional terms, here resolved partially by means of a veritable Zen garden, in which there are a series of seats embedded around the table, as occurs in traditional Japanese houses. The remaining part of the section is occupied by two gardens, almost completely transparent inner courtyards, from which the plants jut out through strategic openings to protrude beyond the glass-paneled shell, so as to integrate the building even more, if possible, into the surrounding wood. The two

72 top The prospect of the inclined, transparent roof is interrupted to allow the growth of the plants in the two small inner courtyards, introduced to integrate the structure even better into the neighboring woods.

72-73 The building was conceived as a greenhouse, constructed with profiles of steel and glass panels, the extreme transparency of which allows the dwelling's inhabitants to live completely immersed in nature.

73 bottom The design of the four faces clarifies how the project resolves into the intersection of a low parallelepiped equipped with screened walls and a taller, transparent prism with a highly inclined profile.

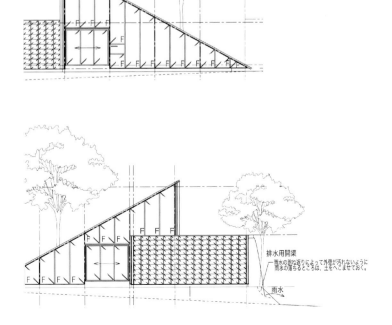

排水用開渠
— 雨水の跳ね返りによって外壁が汚れないように
雨水の落ちるところは、土をへこませておく。

雨水

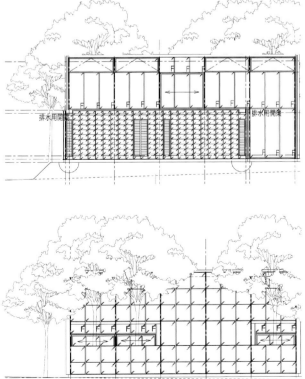

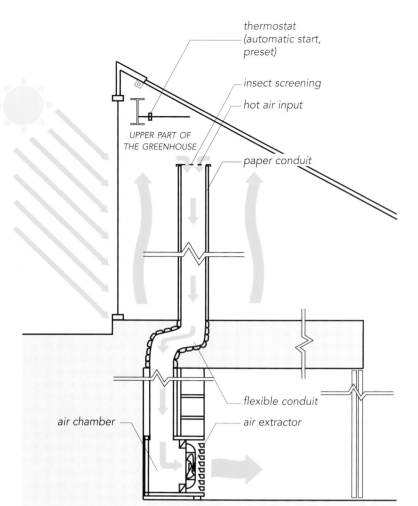

thermostat
(automatic start,
preset)

insect screening

hot air input

UPPER PART OF
THE GREENHOUSE

paper conduit

flexible conduit

air chamber

air extractor

SCHEMA FOR HOT AIR CIRCULATION SYSTEM
*The warm air produced in the greenhouse can be used as a passive heating
system once it is conducted to the bedroom, living room and kitchen.*

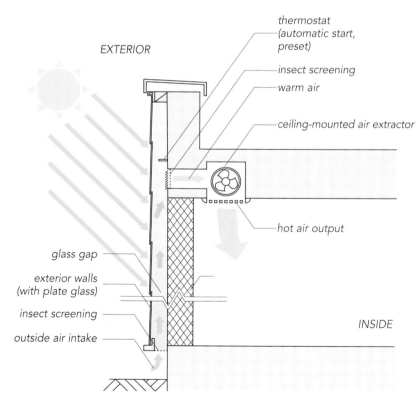

EXTERIOR

thermostat
(automatic start,
preset)

insect screening

warm air

ceiling-mounted air extractor

hot air output

glass gap

exterior walls
(with plate glass)

insect screening

outside air intake

INSIDE

SCHEMA FOR THE WALL
*The plates of glass utilized as external walls allow producing heat in the
interstices, exploiting sunlight by means of the greenhouse effect. In winter,
the warm air thus produced accumulates in the mass of the wall.
When the temperature in the interstice exceeds a certain level,
it automatically activates a sensor to transfer of hot air into the house.*

*74-75 The view toward the exterior from the rooms in the lower
structure is screened by opaque panels positioned inside the
transparent shell, while the higher section of the prism is organized
over two floors through the use of a free-form wooden mezzanine.*

sections of the sitting room, distributed over two levels through
a structure and a staircase in wood, face onto these gardens.
To avoid an excessive entry of light, this section can be screened
on the interior by a series of fabric frames recalling the color of
the interior partitions of rice paper.

The aesthetic coldness of the metal and glass structures
is balanced by the wood and paper structures characterizing
the interiors, as well as by the furnishings of Minimalist imprint
realized using the same natural materials, thus maintaining
direct reference to the Japanese habitational tradition. This
choice, furthermore, renders even more obvious the intention
of building a dwelling that is sustainable from several points
of view.   B.S.

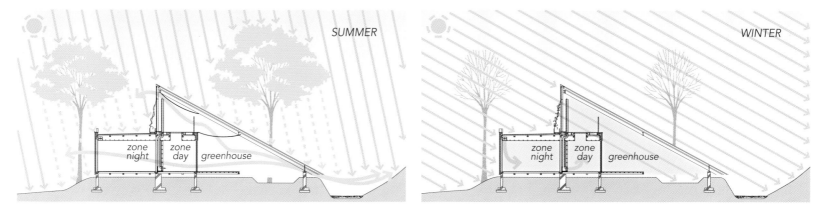

SUMMER

WINTER

zone night | zone day | greenhouse

HEATING OF THE INTERIOR SPACES

In summer, the trees provided shade for the entire building, which has openings in strategic positions allowing the rooms to profit from natural cross-ventilation, removing the warm air accumulating inside. In winter, the trees surrounding the building lose their leaves, allowing sunlight and heat to enter the shell, heating the rooms primarily by passive means.

Bull Bay House

NORTH BRUNY ISLAND, AUSTRALIA

This splendid residence is located on the north coast of the Australian island of Tasmania rising on an 18 ha (about 44 ac) lot characterized by an undulating terrain leading via a steep and craggy path to a beach on the ocean. This magnificent panorama persuaded the commissioning party to favor the ocean view by situating the building so as to have direct access to the beach. Following this aspiration, the project planner decided to situate the constructed body in a dominant position with respect to the ocean, at the remotest and steepest point of the property, suspending part of the constructed body on a natural slope and opening the shell out toward the spectacle of nature.

The client also advanced another essential requirement to the architect: to optimize the building in terms of energy, to reduce operating costs. In order to obtain this result, the most efficient solution was to follow the rules of bioclimatics in designing it, which, in this geographical zone, require orienting the constructed body in such a manner that the locales are struck by sun for the major part of the year, by opening it as much as possible toward the north. The panorama to be enjoyed from the house, however, in this case was oriented toward southeast, that is to say, the opposite side. Faced with this dilemma, the architect chose nonetheless to open the principle rooms of the dwelling toward the

78-79 *The building results from the combination of a glass-paneled section hosting the living room and master bedroom and another portion, more contained, in wood, hosting guest rooms and related facilities.*

78-79 The building results from the combination of a glass-paneled section hosting the living room and master bedroom and another portion, more contained, in wood, hosting guest rooms and related facilities.

79 The transverse sections of the building show how the structure remains partly suspended with respect to the natural incline of the lot, which slopes down toward the ocean.

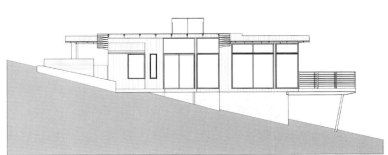

landscape by means of a series of glass fixtures, which he chose from among those best efficient in terms of transmittance. Meanwhile, he advanced the day room with respect to the entire living volume so as to obtain at least one entirely glass paneled locale that would also have a northern exposure, creating in this way the prerequisites for obtaining a series of passive gains useful in reducing the requirement of energy for heating. A large terrace was fashioned in front of the sitting room, which can open almost completely onto the terrace, running all along the "panoramic" side of the dwelling, and suspended, like a good part of the house, on the slope going down to the sea; this is equipped with a light stairway for

access to the garden below and from there to the beach.

The opaque shell, which characterizes the service locales in the guestrooms, directed primarily toward the east and west, is well isolated thermally owing partly to the choice to build the entire structure out of wood. The external shell and the terraces were realized using planks of *Pinus macrocarpa*, a local variety of wood, whereas the coatings for the interiors and the doors use recycled wood as much as possible. The choice to use exclusively this material for the exteriors was made so as to integrate the building into the landscape, as a discrete presence. The majority of the interior walls were plastered and painted white, so as to further emphasize the natural light that enters through the windows.   B.S.

80 center The site selected for the villa is located where one can admire the panorama of the entire bay with a single glance.

80-81 top The building was constructed in a dominant position over the ocean, and conceived so that the sloping profile of the terrain protects it from the gaze of passersby on the street.

80-81 bottom The prospect facing the street includes a courtyard excavated partly into the terrain, ensuring the occupants maximum privacy, even on this side. The alternation of several layers with different profiles allows the natural light to illuminate the interior rooms from above as well.

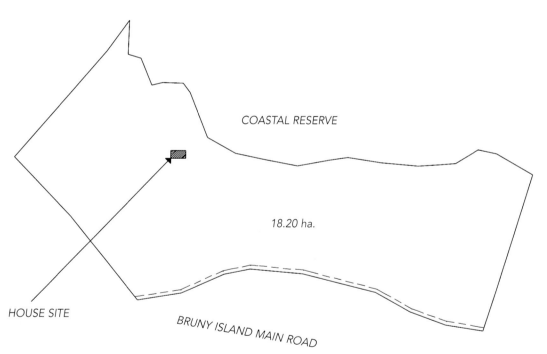

COASTAL RESERVE

18.20 ha.

HOUSE SITE

BRUNY ISLAND MAIN ROAD

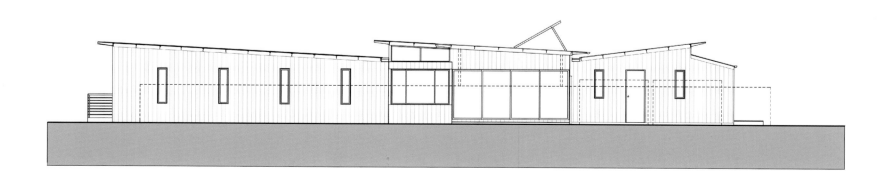

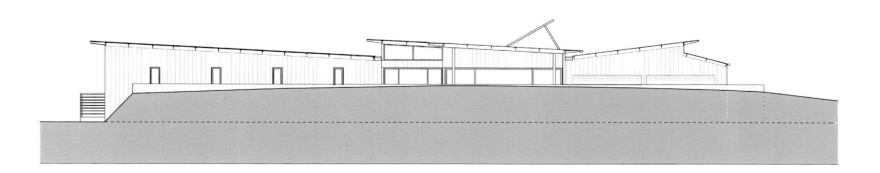

82 top By opening a large glass wall, the living room can be expanded toward the exterior and integrated with the large terrace facing onto the ocean.

82 bottom The plan shows how the house is organized into two distinct parts: one long and sheltered, reserved for guests, and a master section, more compact and transparent, which also captures the view of the ocean and the passive heat of the sun coming from the north.

82-83 The living room provides a very luminous space from which one can enjoy the splendid panorama of the bay, dotted by green trees in the underlying garden.

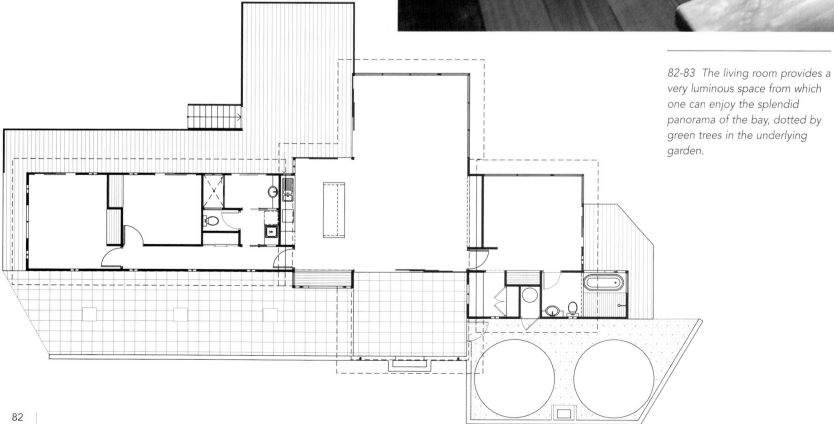

83 bottom The simplicity of the master bedroom is intentional, to avoid distracting the occupants from the panorama visible through its transparent walls.

84-85 The house is oriented to allow appreciation of the best exposure to the sun as well as of an exceptional view of the surrounding mountains and the plain extending toward Lake Constance.

84 bottom Access to the dwelling is from the side facing uphill, where the building emerges from the slope with just one floor, opening less toward the less favorable exposure.

Haus A

KEHLEGG, AUSTRIA

aus A, realized in 2009 in the outskirts of Dornbirn, Austria, represents the most recent landmark in a research itinerary begun some years ago by architects Helmut Dietrich and Much Untertrifaller. Dietrich and Untertrifaller are among the most representative (and famous) practitioners of the "Vorarlberg phenomenon," which has turned the diminutive Austrian region into a reference point for modern architecture.

The experiment that began with the Vorarlberg *baukünstler* movement (the young architects who rebelled against the status quo of the profession beginning in the 1970s) resulted in the cultural, economic, and social revival, and the environmental appreciation of a region at the threshold of a crisis, potentially destined for marginality. With a territory that is 80 percent mountainous, Vorarlberg was forced to reinvent its own future at a time when local industry (textiles, in particular) had succumbed to the blows of globalization. The principles and themes of sustainable development were a powerful engine for change, and architects were among the best and most attentive interpreters. They favored one of the determining processes: innovation by local carpenters, who transformed themselves from artisans to entrepreneurs able

85 top The spaces in the day zone open out onto a broad terrace protected by the protruding façade.

85 bottom The vehicle entry path passes uphill of the building, and from here one can enter directly into the property's access courtyard.

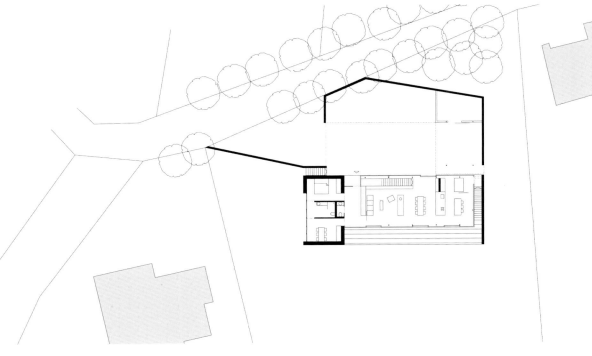

to compete in national and international markets. Today, above all, they are important innovators in wood construction technologies.

Haus A contains many of the elements of contemporary architecture that have made Vorarlberg one of the most frequented destinations for study travel by students and designers. The relationship between the place and its constructional tradition is of paramount importance. Dietrich and Untertrifaller undertook a lengthy operation of re-elaboration, modernization, and "refinement" on a single-family Alpine house, and succeeded in proposing a completely modern version. Haus A settles on the terrain with its primary access parallel to the level curves, providing the best possible exposure in terms of sun and atmospheric and environmental elements. The areas for services, connections, and distribution of various spaces face toward the high vegetation protecting the uphill side of the building. All the living spaces open out onto the better exposed side, distributed simply, with the daytime zone on the upper floor and the nighttime zone on the lower floor. The entire building is heated using a biomass furnace.

The use of the native wood, Vorarlberg white fir, testifies to the close connection the new architecture of this region has established with the local economy. Productive forestation (and, therefore, the conservation and maintenance of woods) and the wood industry today represent one of the principal sectors – together with tourism, service, and agriculture – upon which hinge the development of an Alpine zone that has succeeded in finding its proper position in large-scale global dynamics.

Far from remaining a limited experiment, the work of prominent members of Vorarlberg's architectural avant-garde – from the "fathers," Baumschlager & Eberle, to the youngest disciples, such as Cukrowicz Nachbaur Architekten and Marte & Marte – has become a model for nearby regions: not only those within Austria, such as Tyrol, but also beyond the borders, in Italy, Germany, and Switzerland.   M.M.

86 bottom The kitchen is situated in the east front of the upper level, where natural light is screened by an open cladding of fir fillets.

86-87 The day zone is one vast space, glass paneled on both of the larger sides and in the kitchen, dining area, and living room spaces.

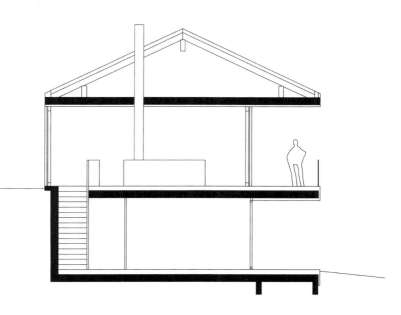

87 top The lower floor is partially recessed into the ground, taking advantage of the slope for insulation.

88-89 The shell of fir fillets is thinner on the east façade, to screen the light without obstructing the view.

89 The structure in reinforced cement covering the parking place connects with the dwelling's copper roof. Uphill, as well, the façade is almost entirely glass paned.

Maison de ville CK06

PARIS, FRANCE

The starting data are what render exceptional the intervention by Franco-Argentine architect Pablo Katz in the 20th arrondissement of Paris (Ménilmontant-Belleville). Finding a vacant plot of land was still vacant within a densely inhabited historic district, and with an excellent corner position, was the first stroke of luck. The opportunity to build a single-family dwelling there was constituted the second element that was decidedly unusual. To make the picture even more interesting, there was the intention, shared by commissioners and project designer, of realizing an architectural work that would be a full expression of its own time: durable, with respect for the environment and well-being for the residents, making use of the best technologies to achieve these goals.

Surrounded by a modest pre-existing constructed area dating from the 19th or early 20th century, the new building contrasts sharply with its environment. Its external appearance

of is that of a cube of glass, steel and wood rising four stories, topped by a welcoming roof garden. The inground floor is made of limestone from quarries in the Paris region; its massive appearance underscores the lightness of the volume on top.

The building's bearing structure is of reinforced cement concrete. The façades have different structures: the one with northern exposure, entirely glass paneled, is of steel; the one facing west is of wood, as is the one facing south – but with larger openings and pierced screenings – toward the interior of the block.

Optimizing the entry of natural light is key to this operation as well as the philosophy of the project planner in general.

In the north façade, transparent and semitransparent parts alternate, providing motivations, for privacy. The part of the shell with wooden structural elements is insulated with a

90 top The roof is an integral part of the dwelling's spaces: a bit of garden and a bit of space for free time and relaxation.

90 bottom The lateral façade is characterized by the contrast between the stone foundation and the wood cladding of the upper floors.

91 Transparent and semitransparent windows entirely cover the principal façade.

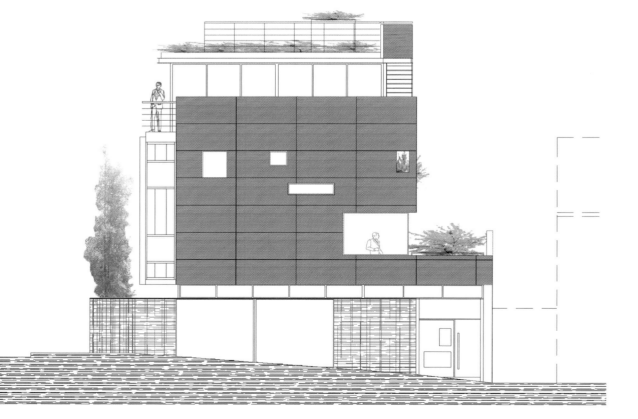

double layer of wood fiber panels; it is coated on the interior with Fermacell insulating panels and on the exterior with cellulose fiber panels with phenolic resin and surfaces in appropriately treated natural wood. Except for the bearing structure of reinforced cement concrete, all materials employed are completely recyclable. But this is only one aspect of an extremely ambitious project that, in the words of the commissioners, should "redefine the scope of what is currently considered possible" regarding sustainable architecture in an urban context. Other "green" strategies unfold for energy efficiency, the management of the building and the comfort of the inhabitants. The optimal insulation of the shell is provided by a floor-based radiant heating system using a gas-fueled condensation heater which in turn integrates an installation of adjustable tubular solar collectors positioned on the cover. A system of double-flow mechanical ventilation with heat recovery, a centralized vacuum cleaning installation, an apparatus for saving water, a system of purifying and recycling gray water, and the welcoming roof garden ensure for project CK06 the highest level of ecological standards.

This complex organism can be managed using the small screens accessible on each floor, which are part of the

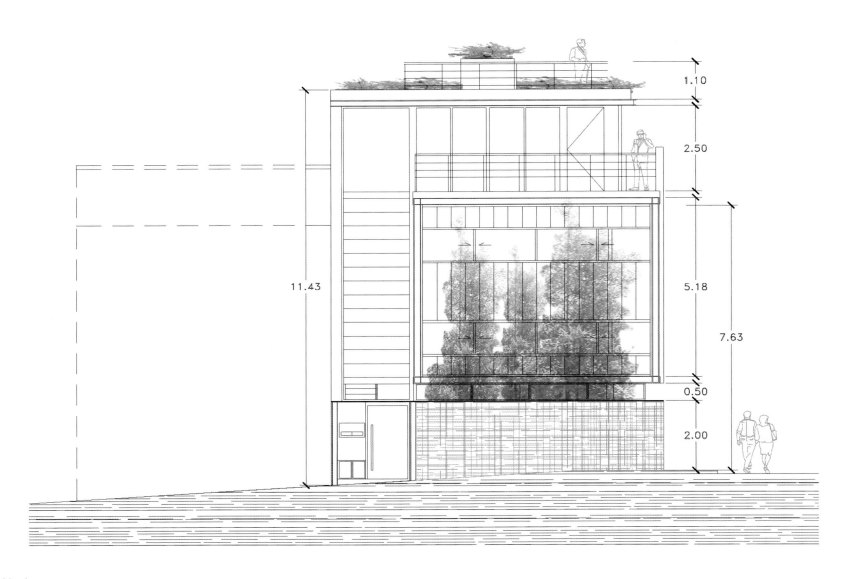

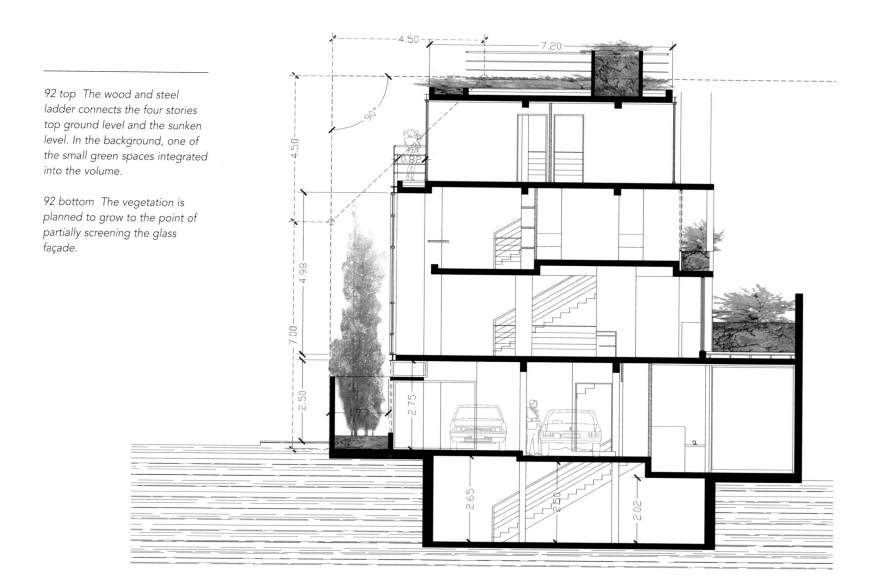

92 top The wood and steel ladder connects the four stories top ground level and the sunken level. In the background, one of the small green spaces integrated into the volume.

92 bottom The vegetation is planned to grow to the point of partially screening the glass façade.

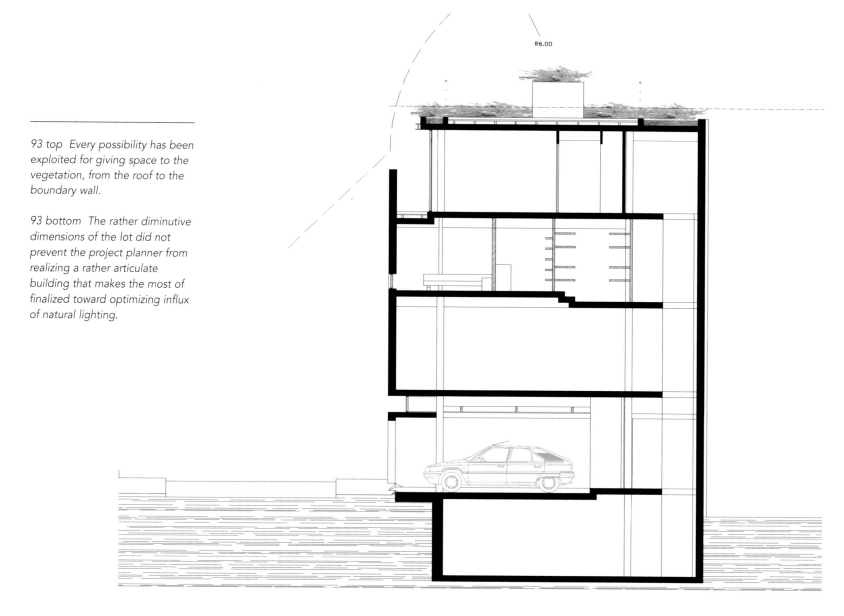

93 top Every possibility has been exploited for giving space to the vegetation, from the roof to the boundary wall.

93 bottom The rather diminutive dimensions of the lot did not prevent the project planner from realizing a rather articulate building that makes the most of finalized toward optimizing influx of natural lighting.

sophisticated apparatus that allows remote control of the heating, the fingerprint scanners at to control opening of the entrance, and the sensors for the artificial lighting system, which can be programmed for a series of predefined scenarios.

The external areas of the dwelling, the courtyard and the terrace on the first floor are scrupulously exploited to maximize the presence of vegetation using innovative techniques. A "vertical garden" system was implemented on the wall separating the property from the adjacent lot and on the wall shielding the view of the terrace from nearby houses. on application of It consists of a textile substratum onto which "pockets" for the plants were applied.

The spectacular conclusion to a stroll through CK06 is the roof garden, outfitted with a basin fed by water heated by solar collectors and covered with a textile structure that can close automatically when the weather warrants.   M.M.

94 top The living room is characterized by the large volume containing the chimney.

94-95 The rough surfaces of the reinforced cement structure left visible contrast with the lightness of the steel structure, the broad glass surfaces, and the wooden flooring.

95 bottom *From the kitchen on the first floor, one can access an exterior space, a terrace embellished with vegetation.*

96 top The lateral and the posterior façades are cladded with cellulose fiber panels, with phenolic resin, and an external layer of natural wood.

96 bottom On the side facing the adjacent property, the façade panels are pierced to ensure privacy for the bathrooms.

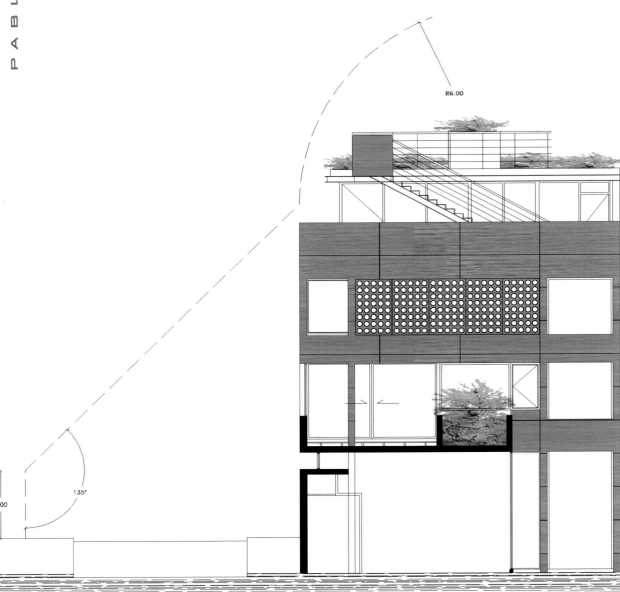

97 Inside, the screening with large circular holes creates a pleasant play of lights and shadows.

Copper Cube
WERDER, GERMANY

A variety of images come immediately to mind with the idea of the "ecological house," among which the most common are a dwelling immersed in nature and a wooden house. The archetype is the cabin in the woods like the one portrayed on the cover of *Walden*, subtitled *Life in the Woods*, by Henry David Thoreau. The baumraum (literally, "tree space") studio, founded in Bremen by architect Andreas Wenning, bases its work precisely on the capacity of the project planner to grasp and give form to a rather widespread, profound desire, that of a refuge in which to lead a simple life in contact with nature. baumraum plans and builds houses in the trees, or, at any rate, immersed among the branches. For the most part, they are small spaces for relaxation, outfitted with simple hideaway beds, but more complex structures have also been realized.

One of them is called Copper Cube, realized in a garden at Werder near Berlin. The dwelling module was conceived as a guestroom near the actual home. Interior furnishings include a double bed and a bench-divan, a bathroom, a closet, and a minibar. All this ensures the guest's autonomy and allows for appreciation, while nestled amid oaks, of the panoramic view of the nearby lake.

By contrast with the smaller units proposed by baumraum , which are attached directly to the tree trunks supporting them, Copper Cube is supported by four steel poles and then anchored to the tree by means of cables of the same material, using also bolts and strips of fabric. Equipped with ample windows facing in every direction, the bedroom also offers a view of the treetops through the skylight in the roof.

Access to the unit is through the first terrace, hanging at 4.5 m (about 15 ft) from the ground; from here a further ramp of stairs leads up to the living module, at 5.5 m (about 18 ft). The shell of the cube was built using a double layer of plywood panels, ventilated and insulated, covered on the inside by oak panels (preference is always given to local wood species) and coated on the outside with copper sheeting. The electrical cables and bathroom plumbing are concealed in one of the four steel support columns.

The livable space is 17 sq m (about 183 sq ft), to which are added the 18 sq m (about 194 sq ft) of the terrace.   M.M.

98-99 top Not a tree house, but rather a house among the trees: Coppercube rises 5.5 m (about 18 ft) from the ground to insert itself among the branches and allow appreciation of the view on the Zernsee.

98-99 bottom The first terrace is at a height of 4.5 m (about 15 ft). From here a second flight of stairs leads to the dwelling unit, a room for guests complete with every comfort.

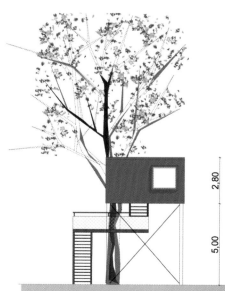

2,80

5,00

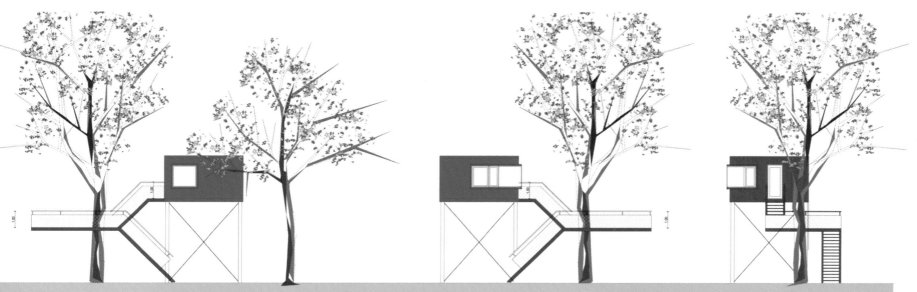

werner sobek *(haus R128)* - walter

hybrid architecture *(cargotecture c32*

- michael hughes *(trailerwrap, little rock*

house) - rintala eggertsson archi

(loftcube) - zen architects *(brunswi*

architects *(passive solar hof house)* - kar

exit architetti associati *(salvaging a*

beauty without waste

unterrainer *(passivwohnhaus L. - E.)* -
) - fabienne gérin-jean *(maison HQE)*
orefab) - single speed design *(big dig*
ects *(boxhome)* - werner aisslinger
lane solar house) - studio granda
witz architecture *(maison passive 95)* -
bià).

beauty without waste

Zero is the new magic number. Zero is the result toward which to strive. A fine reversal of values in a society where more (more growth, more wealth, more consumption) has become a founding myth in itself.

Zero, therefore. And when the objective seems too ambitious, even "almost zero" will work, as stated by the new European directive on energy performance in buildings: all buildings constructed after 2020 must be at "almost zero" emissions; for public buildings, the effective date is 2018.

In Europe, initiatives of the European Commission have smoothed the road regarding energy efficiency and containment of CO_2 emissions in the building sector. But this is nothing other than the most important result of a long process initiated by individual nations, more frequently by individual local administrations, by eco-institutions, and by other organizations for independent research – obviously including those outside the Old Continent, considering that the program most highly accredited on an international level to certify sustainability for a building is the American LEED.

We have been working on energy efficiency in construction ever since the first large-scale oil crisis in 1973, but only recently has it truly become a common language and a widespread reality. In the meantime, however, it has become more complicated to orient oneself among the many and various definitions of a house that "tends toward zero" because it is not only efficient use of energy that counts.

But let us proceed in order, starting with energy, a subject that is emphasized today more than ever. There are many definitions, norms, and standards (whether mandatory or optional); many protocols for certification (and thus many ways of classifying houses on the basis of consumption); and many technologies project planners and builders can use for reference. From the most generic label of a "low-consumption house" (a house that consumes about half of what current norms call the minimum requirement), we pass to more complex prescriptions, such as that for the "passive house," meaning one that consumes fewer than 15 kWh per sq m (about 1.4 kWh per sq ft) per year (in Italy, this value represents less than 1/10th of the estimated average consumption), on to the "self-sufficient"" or "autonomous" house, and even to the plus-energie-haus, a house that produces more energy than it uses.

A variety of names , which corresponding to an even larger variety of project strategies, as illustrated by the examples on the following pages. Even among passive houses, which are subjected to the most restrictive standards from the point of view of technology and project planning, we can find examples that do not appear even remotely related to one another, such as the Passivwohnhaus L. – E., in Feldkirch, Austria, by Walter Unterrainer, made of wood and coated with nothing less than a textile shell; the building by Studio Granda in Skagafjördur, Iceland, made of reinforced cement coated with wood; or her, Maison Passive 95 by Karawitz Architecture in Bessancourt, France, made entirely of wood and glass.

Haus R128 by Werner Sobek in Stuttgart, Germany, in turn, points toward self-sufficiency, utilizing strategies for energy efficiency as well as for exploitation of renewable energies: theoretically, it could even be detached from gas and electricity lines.

As mentioned, avoiding waste of energy is only the first step, and the easiest, in view of the carelessness with which we designed and built in past decades.

Another context in which project designer creativity has been applied with brilliant results is in relation to saving primary materials. In technical terms, we speak of "gray energy," meaning the energy consumed during the phases of production, transportation to place of use, and breakdown of material.

Significant results in terms of material savings have been obtained by applying, for example, the techniques of prefabrication. Dry mounting of components already dimensioned to perfect size in the workshop minimizes discards and reduces enormously the duration of the construction site. A large number of the houses included in this volume have been realized using prefabrication techniques; in the following chapter, there are many examples of prefabricating the entire habitational organism – such as the LoftCube – where the constructional system, and not the object of the construction effort, is produced in the laboratory. Walter Unterrainer's house in Feldkirch was realized using large bearing panels made of wood, produced in the workshop, transported to the construction site, and assembled in very short time; whereas the Little Rock Prefab by Michael Hughes was composed by placing three-dimensional modules side by side.

Along with rendering the constructional process more rational by assembling components that are already perfectly sized, there are other paths for conserving material. As we know, they all begin with the letter R: recycle, reuse, recover, revitalize, rethink, reinvent.

Recycling materials and components from the demolition of other buildings is certainly not a novelty. We need only think of what happened to the Roman ruins during the resumption of urban civilization in Europe beginning in the 10th century. Today the components of a large infrastructure can recall, by comparison with the dimensions of a single-family home, those same "out-scaled" elements that we can observe in cases where the remains of large Roman buildings have been integrated into the more modest urban fabric woven during the Middle Ages. Like what happened with the Big Dig House by SINGLE Speed DESIGN (SsD) in Boston, Massachusetts, where a steel structural module for a highway ramp "contains" the entire house, which develops in its interior.

But smaller objects, also, can be recycled, as in the case of the mobile home that became a small and elegant low-cost dwelling in the Trailer Wrap project by Michael Hughes, or that of transportation containers, the basic modules for global commerce, transformed by HyBrid Architecture into a dwelling and resulting also in the invention of Cargotecture®.

Passing from the R of recycling to the R's of recovery and revitalization, we open an almost boundless field of possibilities and create an immense repertory of projects capable of deriving a work of contemporary architecture, efficient and intrinsically sustainable, from a pre-existing object of building construction. Exemplary in this sense was the intervention upon a traditional building in an Alpine environment, recovered by EXiT Architetti Associati, to transform a centuries-old stable into a sustainable modern dwelling.

Many of the aforementioned projects target yet anotherfurther type of waste, one whose direct and indirect effects have been receiving ever-growing attention in recent years: the waste of space. The continual expansion of urban centers – registered on a global level and witnessed in 2008 by the historical event of the outnumbering of rural populations by urban populations – comes at the price of a massive consumption of soil, which, from natural or farmed land, is turned into constructed ground space.

The real estate bubbles are represented physically by the emptying of historical centers and by the endless bloating of urban outskirts and inhabited centers, which sprawl d into the hinterlands, or conurbations or metropolitan regions whose boundaries are ever more uncertain. The flourishing of projects for small and very small dwelling units represents a reaction to these phenomena of purely "financial" use of ground space. Cargotecture® and Boxhome, and even an intentionally fashion-oriented object like the LoftCube, are statements against the waste of ground space. They tell us that, at times, just a little is enough and that we do not all have to live in houses conceptualized to accord with functional standards and lifestyles that no longer correspond to reality. They tell us it is possible to recover a great number of unutilized spaces in the city, to make them inhabitable by turning them into small, intelligently designed houses.

Zeroing out the waste of space is the most revolutionary of objectives. And among the various "zeros" to pursue, it is the one that can most profoundly change our idea of the house. M.M.

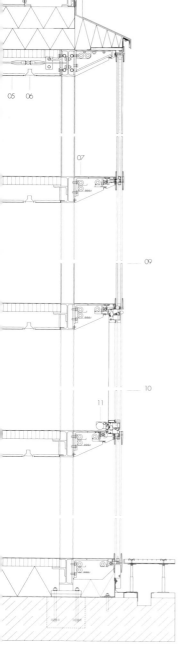

Haus R128

STUTTGART, GERMANY

A veritable demonstration of technological force, Haus R128 represents one of the two opposing poles identified known as low tech and high tech, between which the experiment of architectural sustainability takes place.

Werner Sobek directs one of the most highly esteemed planning and consulting companies operating internationally (with branches in Stuttgart, Frankfurt, Dubai, New York, Cairo and Moscow). He is without doubt one of the best interpreters of high tech.

With Haus R128, realized on the hills surrounding Stuttgart as a home for his own family, Sobek intended to experiment with many of the solutions refined in the numerous projects in which he had participated. From this was born a house-manifesto for the potential of "green" technologies and for the possibilities of sustainable construction, while maintaining canons of the modern language such as free plan, free façade, and maximization of glass surfaces.

The dwelling, erected upon a steeply sloping terrain, is accessed from above, with a footbridge connecting to the street. In descending through the four levels, we find first the daytime zone (entry, kitchen, dining room on the zero level, the highest; living room and studio on level -1), then the nighttime zone (master bedroom on level -2 and second bedroom on garden level -3). The only enclosed areas are the service blocks and certain technical spaces. The system that manages the interior climate and supplies the energy is particularly articulate and based on: the characteristics of the shell (triple glass with film reflecting infrared frequencies to prevent overheating); the use of a surface geothermal plant for preheating and precooling of air; a photovoltaic micro-central (48 modules) on the covering; a system of heating and

104 left The constructional system has a limited number of elements, a choice that enormously facilitates eventual dismantling.

104 top Haus R128 is a cube of glass and steel erected on a slope facing the center of Stuttgart.

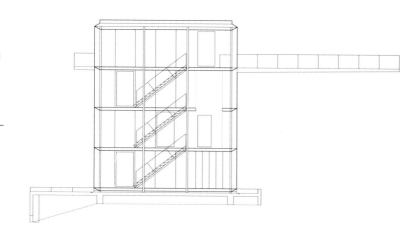

104-105 top *The home is accessed from top, through a long footbridge leading to an authentic panoramic balcony.*

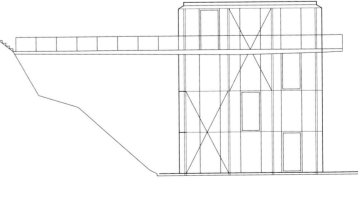

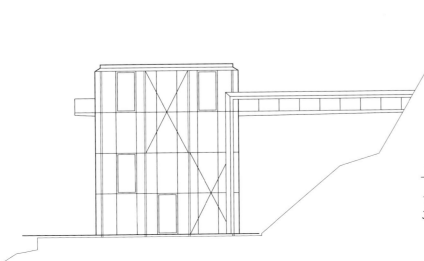

104-105 bottom *The entire building is planned on a module of 2.90 x 3.85 m (about 9.5 x 12.6 ft). The resulting façades are practically identical.*

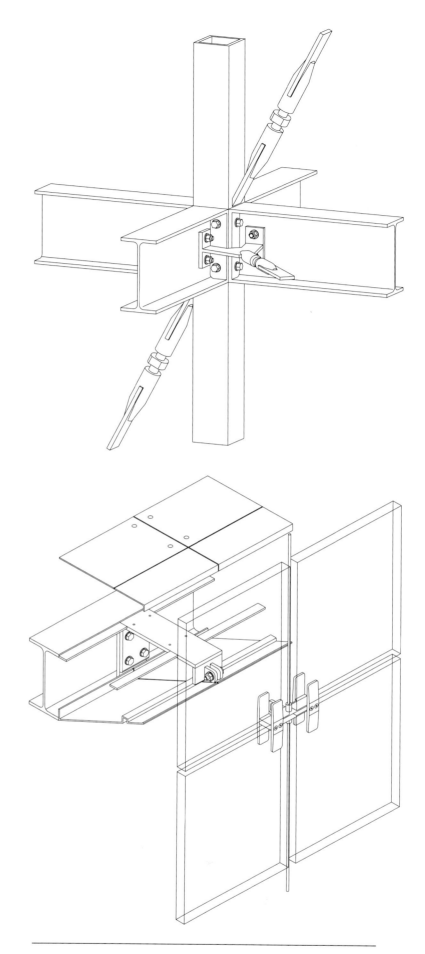

cooling integrated into the false ceilings; a double flow ventilation system with heat recovery; and a reservoir for storing sanitary hot water.

The steel structure was assembled in only four days and then completed using components realized with just a single material – like the aluminum false ceilings and the wooden floors – to facilitate dismantling and recycling.

The transparency of Warner Sobek's crystal cube has a twofold significance: the obvious one, allowing residents to appreciate the spectacular center-city panorama; the other, to make everything visible in a sort of permanent exhibition of the green technology that connotes our future.

Based on the experience of Haus R128, Sobek has refined a project methodology called Triple Zero®, meaning zero emissions, zero energy, zero rubbish. Its characteristics are:

Zero energy: The building must be self-sufficient, using sources of renewable energy located in the interior and on the shell of the building itself, or on the land plot on which it is built.

Zero emissions: The reference value is the total demand of primary energy for the dwelling, converted into CO_2 emissions; no combustion process is permitted, in the building or on the lot.

Zero rubbish: No rubbish must be produced during the process of dismantling or re-converting the building. The terrain must be able to return to its natural state.

A radical approach, finding its complete expression in Haus R128. M.M.

106 top left A metal ladder internally connects the four floors of the dwelling.

106 top right The structure is a grid of 200 mm (about 7.9 in) of steel IPE beams anchored to square-section steel columns 10 cm (about 3.9 in) per side. Steel cables provide support.

106 center The glass façade is detached by 40 cm from the bearing structure. The gap is filled with box-shaped aluminum elements containing installations.

107 A two-story void connects the spaces on the ground level (entry, kitchen, and dining zone) with the living room spaces one level down.

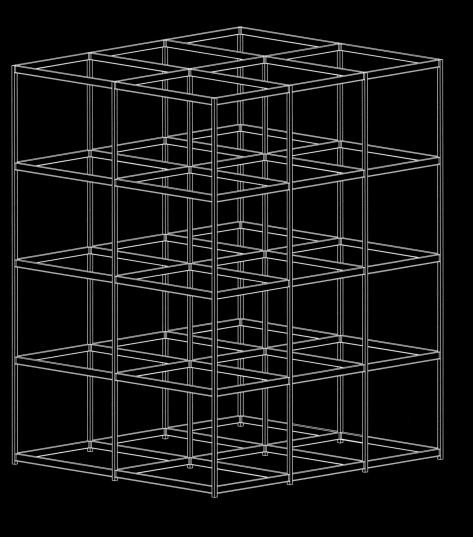

108-109 The steel structure, whose assembly phases are diagrammed in the four images, was bolted together on the construction site in just four days. After the principal structure was erected, the horizontal and vertical shorings were assembled, then the interior metal ladder and, lastly, the elements of the panels for the flooring and roof.

109 top right A view by night reveals the total transparency of the shell. Privacy is ensured by the surrounding vegetation and the house's distance from neighboring properties.

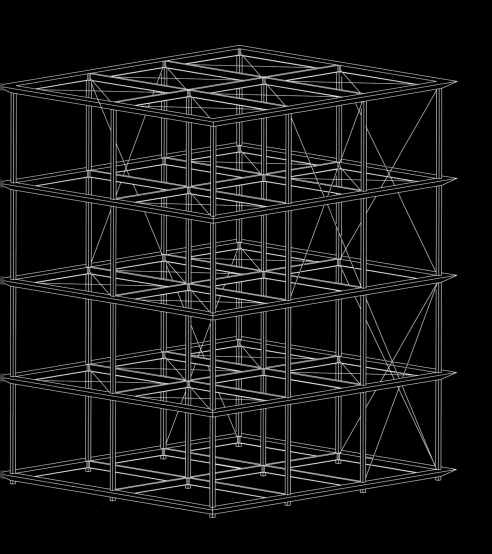

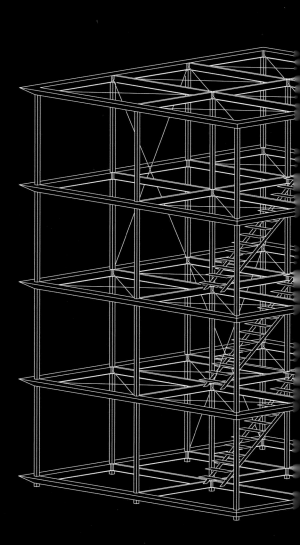

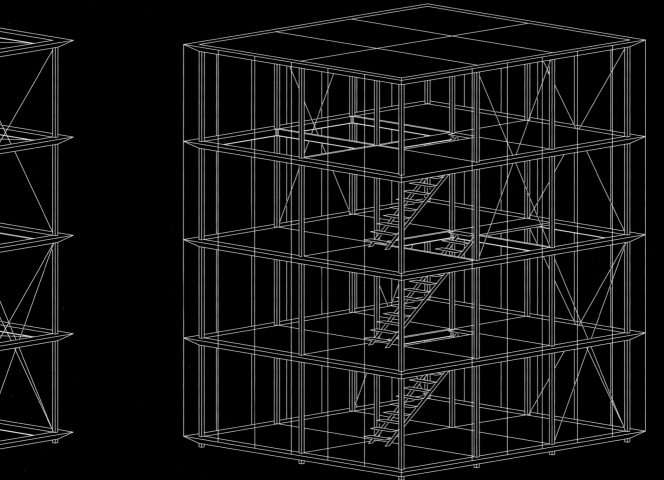

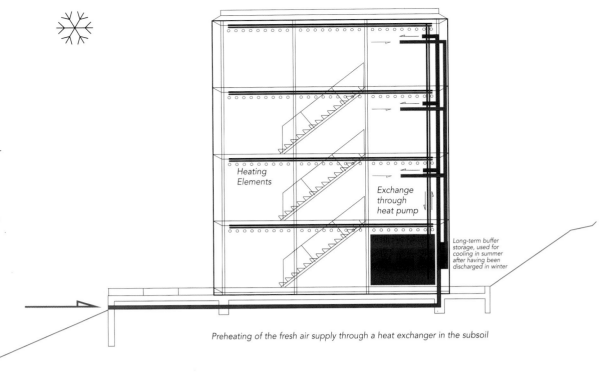

Preheating of the fresh air supply through a heat exchanger in the subsoil

Heating Elements

Exchange through heat pump

Long-term buffer storage, used for cooling in summer after having been discharged in winter

110 top During the cold season, circulation of air is ensured by a geothermal heat pump with a heat exchanger: the outside air is preheated by the ground before entering the living spaces.

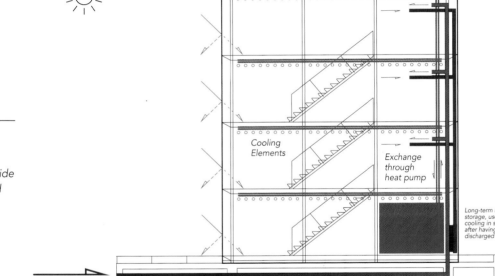

Precooling of the fresh air supply through a heat exchanger in the subsoil

Cooling Elements

Exchange through heat pump

Long-term buffer storage, used for cooling in summer after having been discharged in winter

110 center By day, in the summer, the difference in temperature between the outside air and the ground is exploited to precool air for the interior.

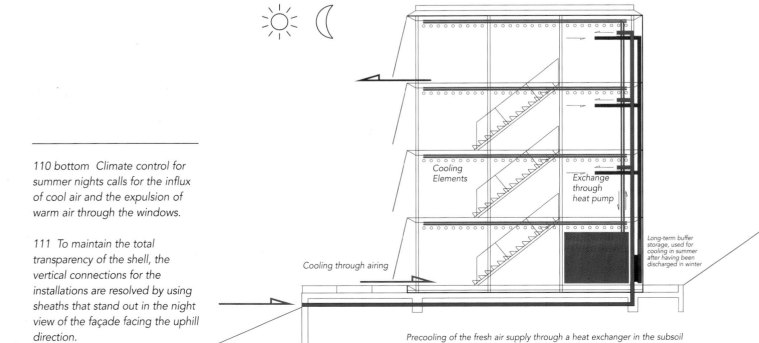

Precooling of the fresh air supply through a heat exchanger in the subsoil

Cooling through airing

Cooling Elements

Exchange through heat pump

Long-term buffer storage, used for cooling in summer after having been discharged in winter

110 bottom Climate control for summer nights calls for the influx of cool air and the expulsion of warm air through the windows.

111 To maintain the total transparency of the shell, the vertical connections for the installations are resolved by using sheaths that stand out in the night view of the façade facing the uphill direction.

Passivwohnhaus L. - E.

FELDKIRCH, AUSTRIA

From poor, marginal territory to veritable "platform for invention" (sustainable, naturally), outstanding, at least on a European level: this is the topical story of Vorarlberg, recently cited in relation to Haus A by by Dietrich Untertrifaller Architekten.

In the Passivwohnhaus L. - E., which stands for Passivhaus Längle-Ess, realized by Walter Unterrainer at Feldkirch, one of the protagonists of the second generation of rebel architects, the *baukünstler*, all the elements can be found that made Vorarlberg's contemporary architecture renowned on an international level, but with something more. Something that recounts how the scenario is still evolving and how research has not cooled into stylistic or technological canons. Walter Unterrainer is a true specialist in terms of containing energy consumption and, in particular, in designing Passivhäuser, according to the standard permitting a maximum annual consumption of 15 kWh per sq m (about 1.4 kWh per sq ft). The Längle home, completed in 2004, consumes only 14 kWh per sq m (about 1.3 kWh per sq ft), meaning less than one-tenth the average consumption of a "normal" house.

How does one achieve such results? Above all, with the correct exposure for the building: the "L" form allows optimization of the southern face, increasing the surface that benefits from best exposure to the sun. The north façade has openings that are very limited, and the service functions are concentrated toward this side, on the ground floor, so as to create an area acting as "micro-climatic buffer" between the living room areas and the wall with the least favorable exposure. The structures higher up, horizontal and vertical, were realized using a system of prefabricated wooden structures of coffers (for the floors) and ossatures, with insulation of insufflated cellulose for the outer walls. The basement, from the floor of the sunken level up to the support for the first-story floor, is of reinforced cement.

But the characteristic regarding this dwelling that strikes most is doubtlessly the external siding, a polyurethane fabric riveted to the structure of the façades, capable of providing protection from water and wind, and resistant to variations of temperature and action of ultraviolet rays. A solution offering a valid and economical alternative to wood and fiber cement siding to "clothe" the houses; an innovative product realized by one of the many enterprises that operate in Vorarlberg in the sector of advanced technologies, which even arose owing to the stimulus provided by the very highly qualified work of architects. Appreciating local resources, therefore, does not mean only utilizing materials that are available on location, but rather knowing how to determine all the opportunities offered by the context. It means entertaining relationships of interchange and of reciprocal fertile influence, with the economy and the society. Even the double-flow system for heating and ventilation is patented by a local company, as are also the triple-pane glass fixtures in larch.

Another important factor in sustainability is flexibility. The interior spaces, as the overall volume arrangement, are easily adaptable to possible changes in requirements of space usage by the inhabitants. The coffer structure for the floors allows large areas of walking space without the need for intermediate supports. This also insures great liberty for modifications of the interior distribution. Over-dimensioning of the structure would also allow the possibility of increases in volumetric arrangements. More flexibility also means greater durability for the constructed organism. The interior walls are constituted of panels of clay coated with plaster, also made of raw earth, and they are easily removable; at the same time, they are capable of functioning as micro-climate control, in particular, for regulation of humidity, a critical element in passive dwellings.   M.M.

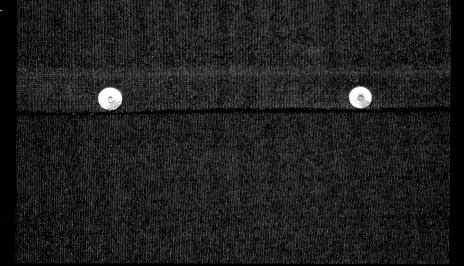

112 top The L-shaped form of the home allows for making the most of the surface with the best exposure to the sun.

112 bottom A shell of polyurethane fabric coats the building, black in order to absorb greatest possible amount of solar radiation.

113 top The textile cladding offers optimal protection from the wind and rain and provides good resistance to temperature variations and ultraviolet rays.

113 bottom The polyurethane fabric utilized by Walter Unterrainereiner is patented by a local company, as are also the triple-pane larch window fixtures.

Cargotecture c320

SEATTLE, USA

Architecture can be produced by using waste material: this is what the creative minds at HyBrid Architecture suggest with their realizations. It is a strong affirmation, sustained by adequate arguments: "HyBrid capitalizes upon the existing; instead of 'reinventing the wheel' with each new project, we prefer to adapt already available materials and technologies to new uses."

Among the many low-cost resources available on the market, the Seattle group has focused on the ISO container: produced in enormous quantities, with dimensions and characteristics that are internationally regulated, it is used for moving wares along the routes of the global economy.

Viewed in a different light, the container has the dimensions and characteristics of a base module, the simple aggregation of which can give form to spaces of widely varying sizes and uses. The container is a "material" capable of defining an approach to an architectural project that is truly unique, to such an extent that it merits a name: Cargotecture®, as the designers have christened it.

The dwelling unit presented in these pages was named c320, where the "c" stands for Cargotecture® and the "320" indicates the habitable surface in sq ft, equivalent to about 30 sq m, obtained by uniting two 20-ft ISO container boxes.

The c320 Studio is thus a minimal dwelling, offering a single person or a couple essential space for living: places for the bed and a piece of storage furniture; a kitchen contained in a piece of furniture; and a micro-bathroom. All the rest, amounting to three-quarters of the total surface, is free space to be used as studio, living room, or dining room.

From the point of view of the worksite, the operation is extremely simple: a foundation in reinforced cement is prearranged, and the container is set upon that. In the case illustrated, the operation was completed with an external wooden platform.

Adequately insulated, the interior of the steel caisson is covered with a care that contrasts, intentionally, with the poor appearance of the exterior. The internal coverings (walls and floor), designed even to the slightest detail, are of plywood with a highly resistant finish, and the details are in stainless steel. The pieces of storage furniture are realized in PaperStone®, a composite material made of recycled paper fiber and phenolic resins.

A hymn to recycling, completed with a green roof that not only improves the installation of the constructed unit but also enhances its harmony with the landscape.

HyBrid Architecture, founded in Seattle in 2003 by Joel Egan and Robert Humble, is an interdisciplinary team of creative minds operating in the fields of architecture, landscaping, history, and urban ecology. Regarding the significance of Cargotecture®, the designers emphasize how the continual growth and expansion of urban populations will pose ever-increasing problems by consuming more and more soil. Cargotecture® addresses the challenge of density while developing models for operating low-cost sustainable housing. The reduced cost is the point of departure for a real democratization of sustainable design, which cannot limit itself to the luxury niche and thus betray its own purposes, allowing urbanization to become a factor in a strong accentuation of inequalities.

According to HyBrid Architecture, "architects have the potential of playing a crucial role in resolving the large-scale challenges posed by urbanization." Their works – the c320 Studio is merely one of the simplest examples – demonstrate that it is not simply a matter of words or fascinating modes of rendering. M.M.

114 The interior furnishings give little or no clue regarding the exterior appearance of the small dwelling unit.

115 The module, consisting of two containers placed side by side and staggered slightly, was situated planned for introduction into the environment with minimum impact during the construction phase.

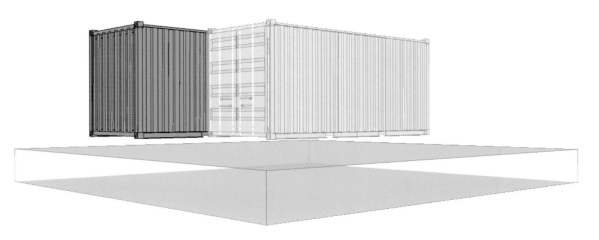

116 top Once closed, the
housing module resumes its
appearance of a "universal"
container for transporting goods.

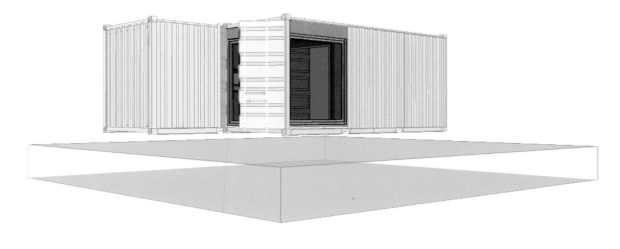

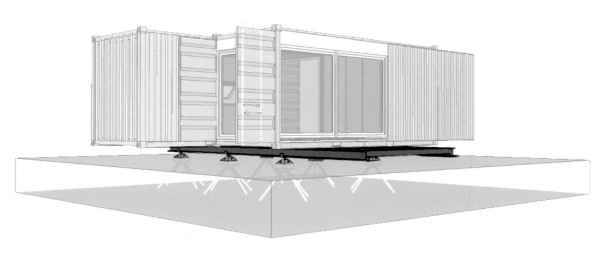

116 center and bottom
The openings were created by
cutting out parts of the original
shell. These were conserved to
function as closures.

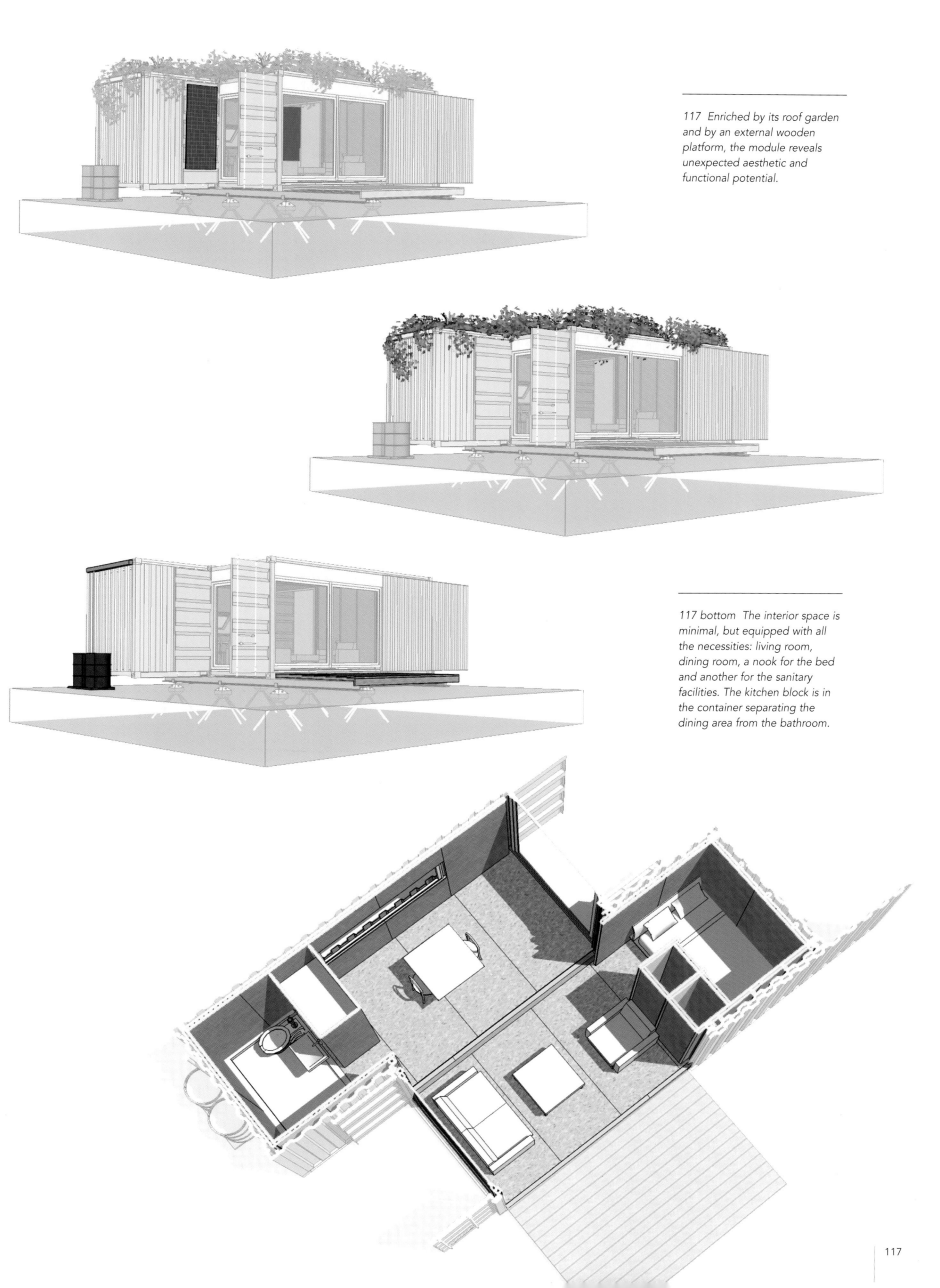

117 Enriched by its roof garden and by an external wooden platform, the module reveals unexpected aesthetic and functional potential.

117 bottom The interior space is minimal, but equipped with all the necessities: living room, dining room, a nook for the bed and another for the sanitary facilities. The kitchen block is in the container separating the dining area from the bathroom.

Maison HQE

TOULON, FRANCE

Among the characteristics that make a house "ecological," up to this point we have placed much importance on the use of local materials, to be reinterpreted and showcased also in terms of constructional techniques. But in the evaluation of a project's sustainability, the parameters we judge by must acknowledge a complexity that leaves little space for simple formulas. The house with swimming pool realized in 2006 in Toulon, in the south of France, on design by Paris project planner Fabienne Gérin-Jean, has merits that might seem to contradict certain conventions of ecological design. The wood used for part of the bearing structure and the external cladding of the dwelling do not belong to the constructional tradition of the place, in this case, Provence. It does, however, present unique characteristics from the point of view of sustainability: it is truly renewable, with a neutral balance of CO_2 and good thermal inertia. It is healthful if chosen with care and not subsequently submitted to treatments with harmful substances. Thus, reasoning in terms of eco-balance, its use is more sensible, and in reference to the French HQE (Haute Qualité Environnementale) scheme for evaluating constructional sustainability, the result is doubtlessly positive. In proposing the use of wood around the Bay of Toulon, a context of typically Mediterranean climate and landscape, the project planner had to overcome the cultural resistance of the local administration. The house is introduced into a constructed fabric characterized by traditional buildings of masonry with layered roofing.

The strategy adopted by the project planner is exemplary in bioclimatic terms: the dwelling is organized over two opposite layers. The spaces facing south enjoy the best exposure to the sun, and are characterized by an open structure of wood and broad glass-paneled surfaces, ensuring interpenetration of interior and exterior. As we proceed toward the interior of the dwelling, and thus toward the north, we find spaces that are more closed and defined by the cement perimeter wall, forming a compact mass acting as a "thermal buffer," practically defining two different buildings: one massive construction with strictly defined spaces, before and upon which a light wooden structure is situated, open and with large open spaces arranged practically in continuity with the exterior. The day zone is essentially concentrated on the ground floor, facing the garden and swimming pool, while the night zone is articulated on the first floor up and the cover level, with an open kitchen conferring a precise functional quality upon this space.

The residents' comfort is ensured, not only by the correct design of the building – and therefore resulting directly from the architecture – but also by the "Canadian well" geothermal installation allowing precooling or preheating of interior air.

To bring to completion his "transplant" of a work of contemporary wooden architecture into a place with different constructional traditions, Fabienne Gérin-Jean had to obtain the necessary technical expertise in a sector outside of building construction: nautical construction. Close up, the large terrace acting as cover to the house doubtlessly recalls the bridge of a large sailing vessel.

The result today is that many more realizations of wooden houses have been built in this region, and a new line of construction is experiencing significant development in the south of France. M.M.

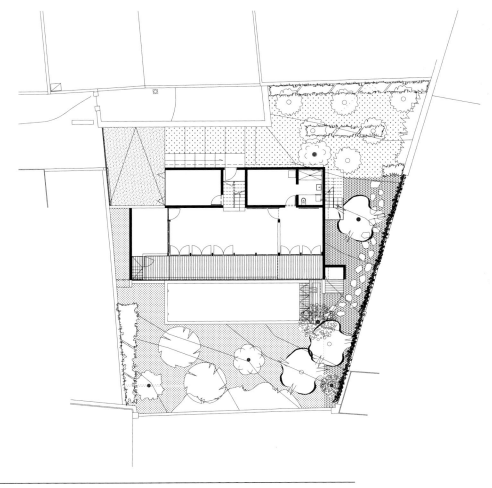

---

118 A wooden house in Provence? To realize this dwelling, the project planner had to challenge cultural conventions and seek the necessary technical competencies in the nautical sector.

119 The house is installed on the lot with a clear bioclimatic strategy: large openings toward the best exposure to the sun and toward the pertinent open spaces, more closure on the opposite side.

FABIENNE GÉRIN-JEAN

TrailerWrap

BOULDER, USA

Michael Hughes is an architect dedicated intensely to teaching. He received his degree from Princeton and has taught at various universities, including the University of Colorado at Denver. While there, he transformed a dilapidated mobile home in a workshop with students.

In the United States, for some retired persons and low income families, trailers still represent the possibility of accessing, at extremely reduced costs, a long-term dwelling that one can own or rent. These prefabricated mobile homes – with low taxes (initially they were treated like vehicles!) and the possibility of being placed on rented lots – became enormously popular beginning in the 1960s, and today the United States has over 30,000 trailer parks, agglomerations of mobile homes that look more like parking lots than actual settlements. Further, like automobiles, trailers depreciate rapidly, and their presence is often seen as having a negative impact on the value of nearby houses. The construction and dwelling quality of these modules is, for the most part, modest and unlike those of an "actual" residence.

Michael Hughes's work with the students at the University of Colorado focused on bringing new aesthetic and environmental values to this type of dwelling: in particular, increasing the living space, optimizing the amount of natural light, and improving energy efficiency. Overall, he aims to explore the possibility of developing a livable, economical model of dwelling for the future.

The point of departure was recycling a 1965 trailer that was already out of use and in a very bad state. The superstructure was dismantled and the steel chassis was kept, later to be reutilized as the foundation for the new home. Foundations and reinforced cement replaced the wheels to give greater solidity to the whole once the chassis was repositioned on-site.

All salvageable material from the dismantling was recycled. A light steel structure was constructed on the free platform, and upon this was placed an ample wooden covering with an inclined layer, again using reclaimed material. The overhang and geometry of the new roof increase protection from the weather and create space for a band of glass at the upper part of the façade, allowing natural light to flood the interior, which, in turn, was reorganized into an elegantly optimized open space.

The new arrangement of the interior allowed the fashioning of an ample veranda screened by a coating of wooden fillets. To ensure energy efficiency, the new shell was realized with walls made of bales of hay inserted into a wooden frame, then covered with plywood panels.

By using inexpensive or reclaimed materials and low-costbuilding techniques, the University of Colorado students (who participated materially in the construction) demonstrated how to intervene and render even lower-quality dwellingssustainable, healthful, and functional, and to impart to them a formal quality that can even be remarkable.   M.M.

120-121 On the chassis of an abandoned mobile home, the team of students from the University of Colorado, coordinated by Michael Hughes, realized a prototype for a low-cost ecological house.

121 bottom A good deal of recovered material, such as the wood for floors, doors, and windows, was utilized to set up the interiors.

Big Dig House

LEXINGTON, USA

The Big Dig House is one of the most curious examples of reusing an existing structure, not only for the type of material that was reused, but also for the final result, a residence of remarkable merit.

The Boston Big Dig is the complex of tunnels by means of which Interstate 93 bypasses the city center. This "great work" has been the object of polemics because of disproportionately rising costs as well as financial and political difficulties that added to the already significant technical and environmental problems. A colossal construction site with great impact, in the eyes of the project designers at SINGLE Speed DESIGN (SsD) it was a veritable mine of materials to be reutilized.

In the Big Dig House, the concept of recycling was pushed to the limit, including even the complete reuse of a support module for a highway ramp. It was not a matter of extracting material to be re-elaborated and modified from the demolition of the infrastructures, but rather of taking a piece of the highway just as it was and transporting it to the site where the house was to be erected.

In this manner, the realization of the principal structure required only two days: once the pieces of the foundation were constructed in reinforced cement concrete, the reclaimed steel structure was implemented in less than 12 hours. Subsequently, the building was completed using the same constructional methodology as that of a prefab house, with the assembly of other large, reclaimed "pieces" such as the slabs of reinforced cement and steel that had constituted the support for the road level, and which became the interior floors and slabs for the

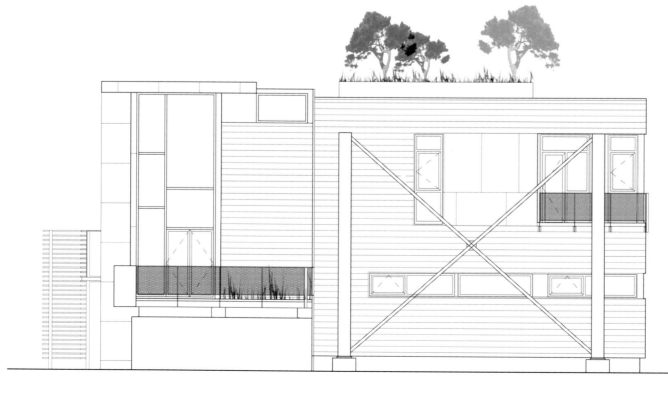

122 bottom The geometry of the façade successfully integrates the recycled steel structure.

122-123 The large steel framework sticks out from the east façade between the wooden surfaces and the ample glass-paneled zones.

123 bottom On the north façade, the protruding steel structure recovered from the Big Dig site anchors an anchorage for the external stairway leading to the roof garden.

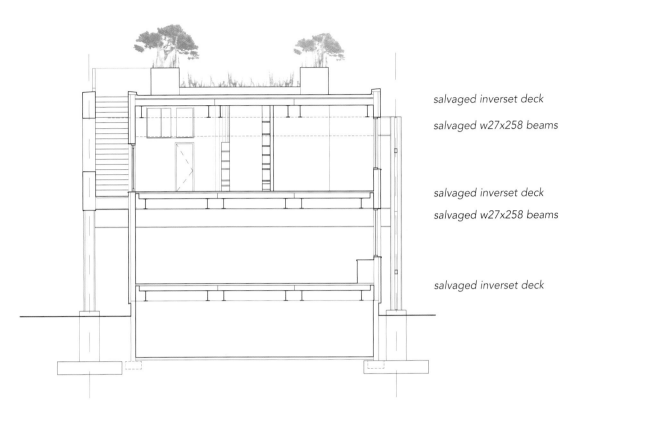

salvaged inverset deck

salvaged w27x258 beams

salvaged inverset deck

salvaged w27x258 beams

salvaged inverset deck

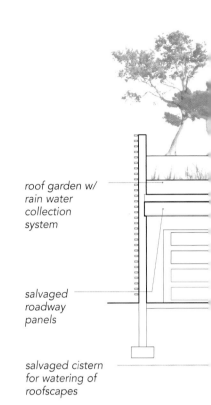

roof garden w/
rain water
collection
system

salvaged
roadway
panels

salvaged cistern
for watering of
roofscapes

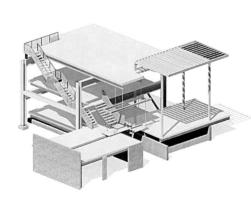
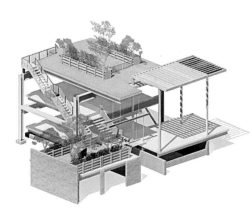
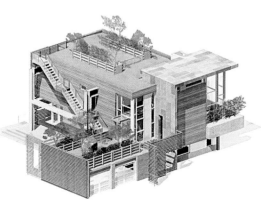

124 top The size of the structure salvaged from the highway yard, highlighted by the outsized plinths of the foundation, are so large that they can almost entirely contain the dwelling.

124 bottom After having realized the plinths for the foundation and certain cement works, the large steel framework was transported to the construction site and used again. Then the horizontal tiles, also recovered, were positioned and the structure was completed with vertical connections, shell, and interior partitions.

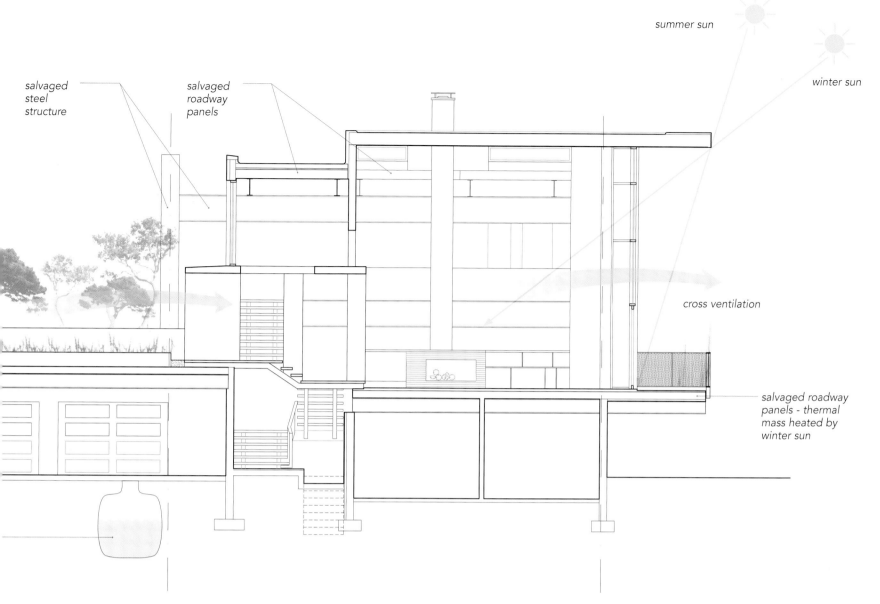

salvaged
steel
structure

salvaged
roadway
panels

summer sun

winter sun

cross ventilation

salvaged roadway
panels - thermal
mass heated by
winter sun

cover. Because these were elements of bearing capacity, decidedly outsized with respect to what is necessary for a home, it was possible to realize a luxuriant garden on the roof. This effectively performs its role in thermal insulation for the interior spaces, and for drainage of rain waters, channeled into a dedicated reservoir.

The house develops over two floors, plus the roof garden: on the ground floor, the day zone; on the upper floor, the night zone, with two bedrooms, closet and double bath. The interior space is rather articulate, with a double volume corresponding to the living room, enhancing the outsized dimension of the steel beams positioned in support of a former roadway slab, now a ceiling.

For the exterior, the SsD architects realized a refined play of contrasts between the rough appearance of the steel megastructure and the elegance of the wood and glass surfaces. The perimeter walls were erected using panels recycled from the Big Dig construction site: components made of a jumble of cement and aluminum, which normally would have been impossible to recycle. But used in this manner, they prove to have an optimal insulating capacity, to the extent that

the house can be heated using a radiant floor system.

Behind this operation is one of the most interesting teams of emerging young project designers on the East Coast of the United States: SINGLE Speed DESIGN studio, founded in 2001 by Jinhee Park and John Hong. For the two architects, sustainability requires an inclusive approach, in which all necessary disciplines converge and collaborate to limit waste of materials, rather than producing a complex methodology in which each contribution is added to the other word of the day Their motto is: minimize use of materials and energy and maximize performance.

The multiple advantages of a correct project methodology emerged from the Big Dig House experience. It led the two architects to continue using e a true project of reuse of pieces of the former structure of the old tract of Interstate 93 to build architectural complexes destined for public use, such as schools, libraries, or social clubs – all structures that can be realized when an infrastructure is demolished, avoiding waste of resources, energy, and, in the final analysis, contributors' funds. M.M.

124-125 The dwelling spreads over two floors plus a sunken level. Among the various "recycled" components is a cistern that collects rainwater to be used for irrigating the green roofs. The bioclimatic strategies adopted point to passive exploitation of heat from the sun, owing to the large glass windows on the south façade corresponding to the double volume, and to the natural cross-ventilation in the interiors.

126 Interior space is distributed
over various levels, connected by
a stairway with the steel
structure.

127 The roof of the garages was
transformed into a hanging
garden, accessible from the living
room.

LEGEND

1 *asian garden*
2 *bridge*
3 *open to below*
4 *library*
5 *office*
6 *master bath*
7 *master bedroom*
8 *terrace*

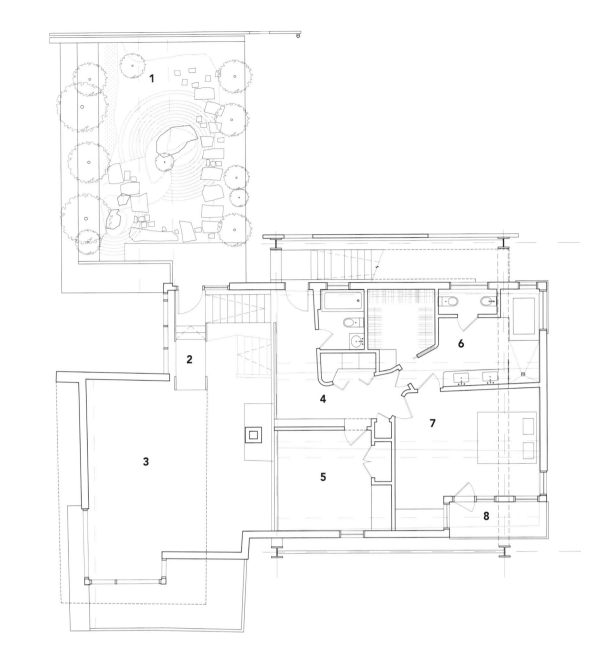

128 top The upper floor of the dwelling, facing onto the double volume of the living room, hosts the master bedroom, with the related service facilities and a studio.

128 The kitchen, dining area, and billiards table occupy one large single space, one level bottom the living room.

129 Corresponding to the living room, the interior volume has double height, allowing one to grasp the exaggerated dimension of the recovered structure.

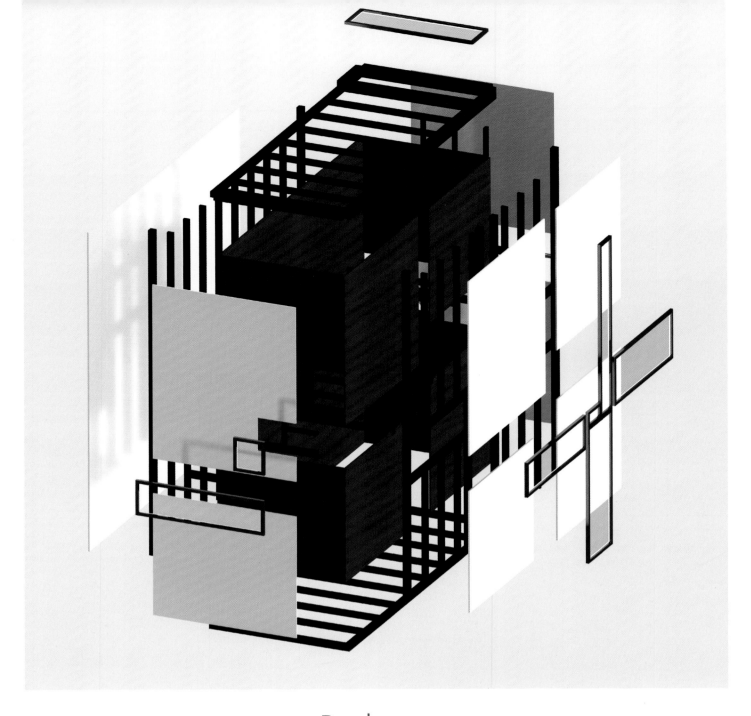

Boxhome

OSLO, NORWAY

Designed by Finnish architect Sami Rintala in collaboration with Icelandic colleague Dagur Eggertsson and Norwegian artist John Roger Holte, the experimental living module known as Boxhome represents a denouncement of the vogue for constructing excessive spaces, often ignoring people's real needs with an eye to maximizing the profits of real estate operators. The designers believe that housing sector regulations limit the possibilities for creating smaller living spaces with economic and environmental advantages. Homes catering to an upscale standard of living often make us lose sight of a dwelling's primary function: to welcome families and protect them from the outside world. Today's construction industry accounts for a third of the energy consumed in Europe and also requires an enormous amount of various materials. Thoughtful use of resources is especially important in northern Europe, where the harsh climate demands energy to heat buildings more than half of the year. Smaller homes are also more economical to manage.

The project's designers refer to the *Existenzminimum* (subsistence dwelling) research conducted in the 1920s by Viennese architect Ernst May, remarking that by reducing and optimizing living space, it is possible to shift the emphasis from quantity to quality while showcasing natural materials and

---

130 The axonometric view shows how the building is composed of only three materials: a central portion in wood and a coating of aluminum sheets, interrupted by elements in glass, ensuring entry of natural light.

131 The external coating of aluminum bestows a futuristic aspect upon a construction realized exclusively in wood: fir for the structure, cypress for the interior coatings, and birch, red oak, walnut and red fir for the furnishings.

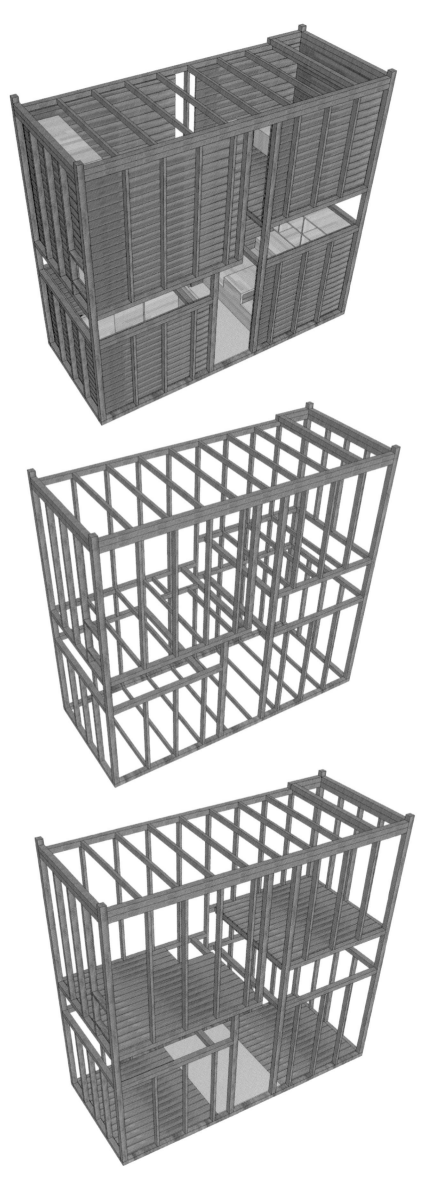

lighting. Based on these premises, a module was designed measuring 19 sq m, distributed over various levels inside a parallelepiped having a base of just 2.3 m by 5.5 m, with a height of 5.78 m. The four interior spaces satisfy the primary requirements for living: kitchen/dining room, bathroom, living room and bedroom. The module, inside its aluminum shell, is constructed entirely of wood: the structure is made of fir, with the outer coverings in cypress; birch is used for the kitchen, red oak for the living room, walnut for the bedroom, and red fir for the bathroom. Reducing and rationalizing the living space, using wooden elements that were standardized as much as possible, allowed Boxhome to be built for a quarter of the cost of comparable homes in the area. The designers believe this prototype, conceived to meet the needs of a single person or a young couple, can be adapted to accommodate larger families or create work spaces.   B.S.

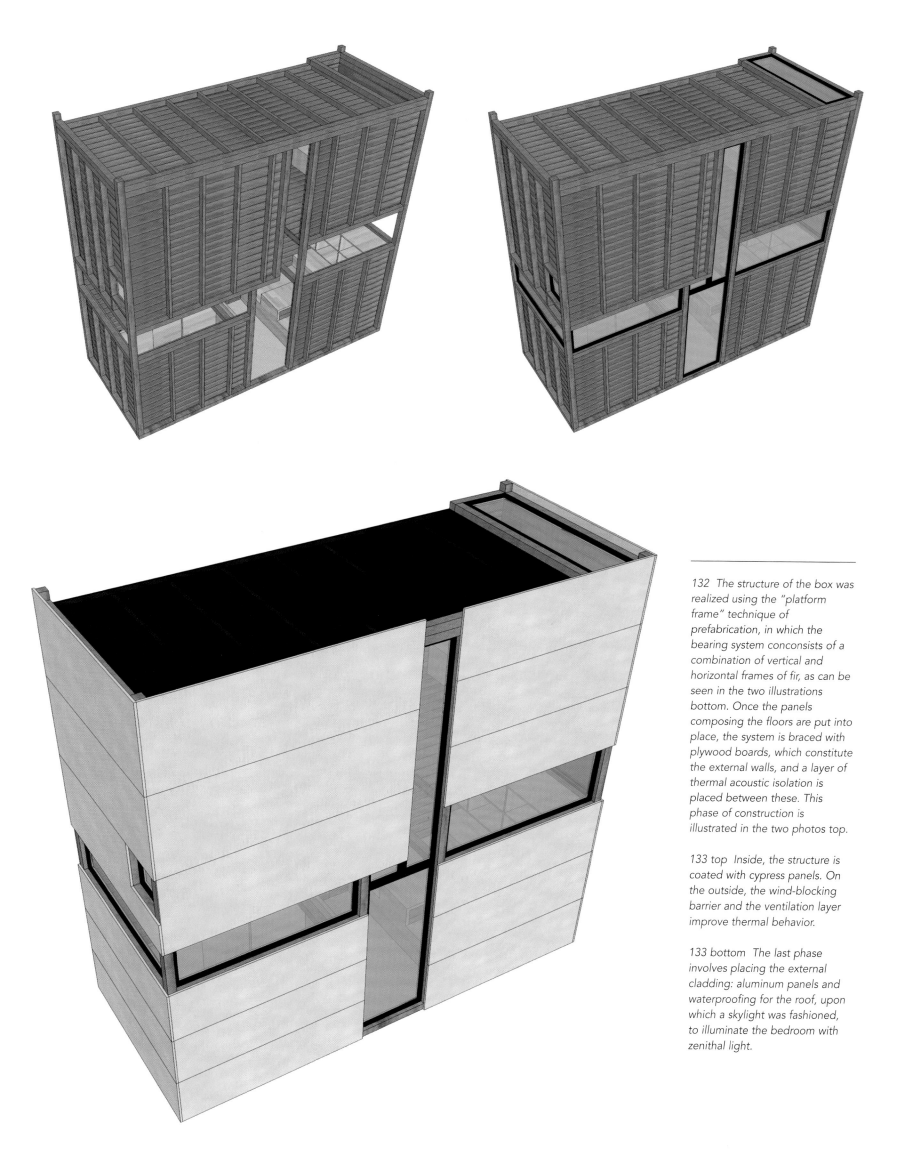

132 The structure of the box was realized using the "platform frame" technique of prefabrication, in which the bearing system conconsists of a combination of vertical and horizontal frames of fir, as can be seen in the two illustrations bottom. Once the panels composing the floors are put into place, the system is braced with plywood boards, which constitute the external walls, and a layer of thermal acoustic isolation is placed between these. This phase of construction is illustrated in the two photos top.

133 top Inside, the structure is coated with cypress panels. On the outside, the wind-blocking barrier and the ventilation layer improve thermal behavior.

133 bottom The last phase involves placing the external cladding: aluminum panels and waterproofing for the roof, upon which a skylight was fashioned, to illuminate the bedroom with zenithal light.

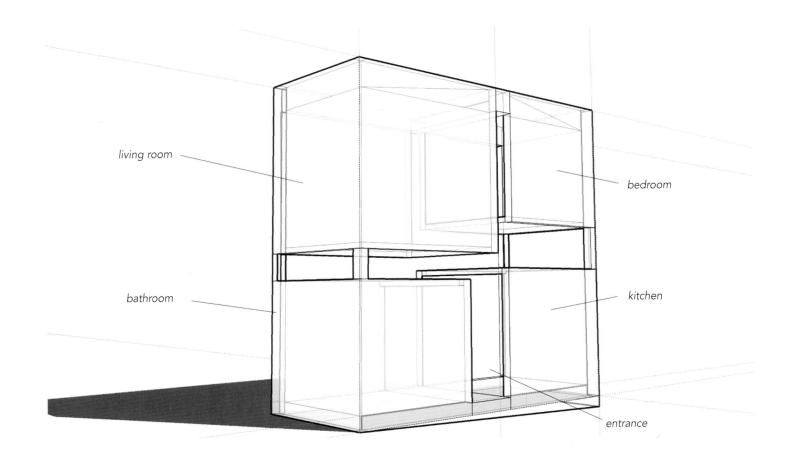

living room

bedroom

bathroom

kitchen

entrance

134 top The "box" contains four rooms in little over 73 cu m (almost 2600 cu ft): entryway, kitchen, and bathroom are on the ground floor; on the upper level, slightly staggered, are the living room and bedroom.

134 bottom left The kitchen table is integrated into the house structure and includes two burners for cooking food according to Korean tradition, with each diner preparing his own meal at the table.

134 bottom right The bathroom is completely paneled in red fir and illuminated through the windows positioned in the upper part, as well as through a simple fluorescent tube on the wall.

135 The bedroom is furnished in walnut and outfitted with a bedside table. From here it is possible to see the living room, from where, in turn, one can glimpse the kitchen through the hole with a climb up and down the ladder at its center.

LoftCube

MILAN, ITALY

Presented for the first time in 2003 at the Berlin Design Fair, LoftCube is the most celebrated example of a long series of minimal habitat prototypes with high technological and comfort standards. In recent years, interest for this type of dwelling has been constantly increasing, giving life to a sector unto itself, defining a context of project planning midway between architecture and design.

The prefabricated al micro-modules, more or less luxurious, more or less "ecological," incarnate a highly diffuse dream, that of a self-sufficient nest, built without particular impact and without all the complexities (and costs and delays) of typical construction, in the desired place.

But how does sustainability fit into the picture? Quite well,

because the idea of prefab al housing modules that can fill in the unutilized spaces of cities is one of the most fascinating paths architects can take to reduce the expansion of urban blight. Of the many possibilities, LoftCube "takes aim" at the flat roofs of modern buildings, formulating a hypothesis to oppose the consumption of soil and the waste of potentially useful spaces. This approach also favors lightness, a way of occupying space without marking it profoundly or permanently. Lightness, impermanence, reversibility of transformations: just as it has been brought on-site, the the micro-module can be removed to restore the place to its original condition.

Among the many proposals elaborated on this particular theme, LoftCube, designed just after the turn of the millennium by Berlin designer Werner Aisslinger, stands out because it proposes an actual dwelling rather than pavilions for specific uses like reading, study or relaxation.

What this housing module of 39 sq m (about 420 sq ft) promises is attractive: just three days to erect a complete dwelling including interior furnishings. Upon a structure of galvanized steel, the façades are realized in wood using thermally and acoustically insulated timber frames. The remainder of the external shell is in glass-reinforced plastic. Almost every detail can be customized: from the number, size, and arrangement of the openings, to the choice of flooring, on to the interior distribution. Thus, one can have a mini-dwelling completely furnished with outfitted walls designed by Werner

Aisslinger himself, or, uniting the modules by means of the special prearrangements, one can habitational organismcreate a more spacious home.

If, in its choice of materials, construction, and installation technologies, LoftCube does not present salient characteristics of sustainability, its "green" evolution is already in place: FinCube is the "natural" version of the hyper-technological and metropolitan LoftCube. Materials and technologies change, but the desire to satisfy remains the same, that of the home nest, warm and welcoming, from which it is possible to observe the outside world, whether a tranquil natural landscape or the most frenetic urban environment.   M.M.

136-137 A complete home in just 39 sq m (about 420 sq ft); LoftCube represents the "fashion" version of the dream of the self-sufficient nest.

137 top Sophisticated automatic systems regulate the management and functioning of these refined, prefabricated micro-habitats.

137 bottom In a project situated somewhere between architecture and design, the interior setup of the LoftCube is realized in part using specially designed elements.

Brunswick Lane Solar House

MELBOURNE, AUSTRALIA

The project was realized to grant an unusual request from the owners of a small demolition lot in the courtyard of a historical building facing onto a bluestone lane. On a strict budget, they wanted a residence for themselves on this tiny lot in spite of a very reduced budget. Besides these limitations, the project designers had to deal with a series of normative constraints imposed by the project's extreme proximity to a heritage house with protected status, and by certain rigid fire safety rules related to the fact that they were constrained to build on three sides of the lot. To resolve all these obligations, they conceptualized a building that could optimally exploit bioclimatic principles, reducing to a minimum the costs of energy needed to operate the dwelling.

The residence is organized on two levels, each with a surface area of 77 sq m (about 830 sq ft), even allowing space for a small interior courtyard. The building seems much larger than it actually is, on account of an innovative arrangement of the spaces and of the presence of numerous external exposures on the three sides, conferring upon it an extreme luminosity.

In observance of local building regulations, a garage was fashioned on the ground floor, in which open-view installations had been previously arranged to allow for the option of transforming it into an additional bedroom and bathroom should the residents decide to forgo the use of an automobile. T a manner the optional extra room would be added to the other two bedrooms and the bathroom already present on the ground floor. The upper level was structured as an open space containing living room, dining area and kitchen. This unusual distribution was chosen to make use of a greater mass to protect the bedrooms from street noise and climatic variations, as well as to ensure the living room a street view guaranteeing both privacy and maximum illumination. This space can thus embody a broad glass-paneled surface exposed primarily toward the north,

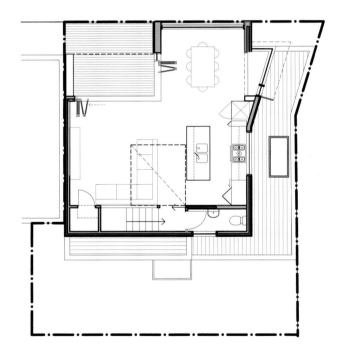

138 left The façade on the street resolves into a series of volumes with different depths, which correspond, in turn, to alternating open and closed spaces.

138 right The first level was resolved with an open space containing the living room, dining room and kitchen. During the warmer season, it extends outward toward the open air by means of the terrace to the north.

139 The bedrooms are arranged on the ground floor, facing onto a small garden. Protected from the street by a wooden fence, it also functions as an entry courtyard.

so as to receive heat from the sun in winter, along with a great deal of natural light. Much of the transparent surface can open completely out toward the terrace, providing an extension to the living room during fair weather, and screened by a wooden trellis blocking the view from the outside. The windows can be opened and are protected by an extension of the inclined roof, which takes the form of a wooden sun-break, calibrated so as to allow the sun's light and heat to enter the living room on colder days and to create an effective screen on hotter days. The strategy for passive cooling is completed by the design of the section, which exploits the chimney effect produced by the inner, double-height stairway, allowing hot air originating on the ground floor to escape through openings above.

Thermal solar panels power a special thermal conductor for heating and dehumidifying interior spaces. In addition to this, a battery of photovoltaic panels was installed on the roof. The combination meets most of the electrical needs of the residence, which is equipped with low-consumption lamps and appliances. There is also a system to recover rainwater to use in the laundry room and for flushing toilets. Gray water is used to water the garden. B.S.

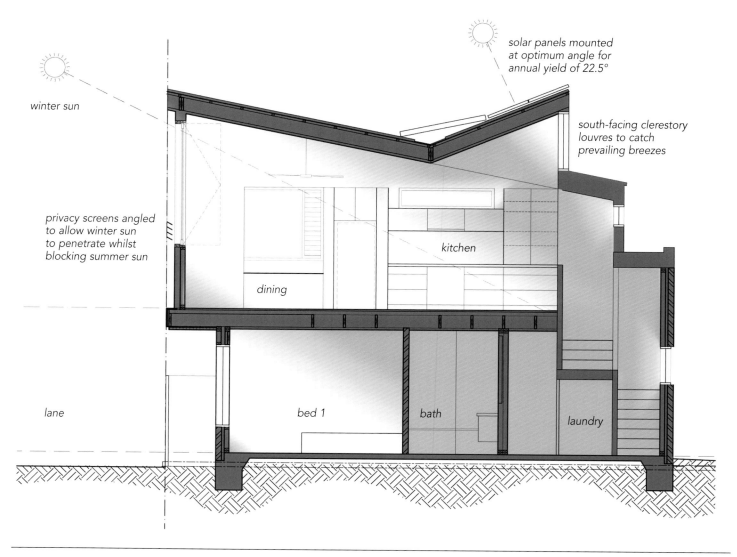

140 top The stairway leads natural light down to the lower floor by means of some windows opening at the upper part.

140 bottom This section reveals how the arrangement of openings

and layers of the roof allows natural illumination throughout the first floor.

141 In summer, the living room extends outward toward the terrace by means of sliding windows, ensuring maximum openness.

Passive Solar Hof House

SKAGAFJÖRDUR, ICELAND

The residence is surrounded by a scenario typical of the Icelandic fjords, into which it integrates perfectly from the climactic and landscape point of view, by adopting the profile and colors of the surrounding nature. Its remote location and the uniqueness of the undertaking required a close collaboration among commissioner, architects, and builders, and this proved fundamental for the successful outcome of the project. The building is part of a small complex that already included another dwelling, a church, a barn, a series of stalls, and a structure for equitation. With respect to these pre-existing structures, the new constructed body remains separate, rising at a dominant position that allows best enjoyment of the natural panorama. The constructional materials employed are, for the most part, of local origin and include also recycled elements, such as telegraph poles, utilized to screen the sunlight, and basalt blocks, taken from excavations for the foundations, which became steps or cladding elements for the floors. Even the grass growing on the roofs comes from the very earth that was dug to make way for the construction.

The form of the building recalls that of the vernacular local architecture, resolving into a succession of volumes of various depths, each characterized by a differently inclined profile. These are composed so as to form a series of skylights in the central section allowing zenithal natural light to enter even

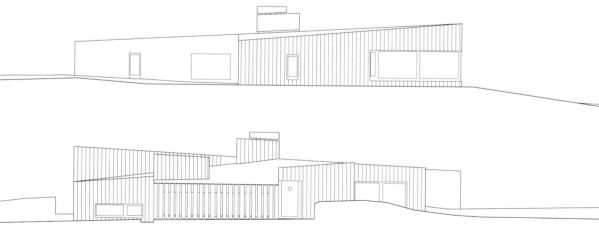

142 top The building is situated on an Icelandic fjord. Its large glass windows facilitate passive solar energy gains and admiration of the surrounding panorama.

142-143 The dwelling displays into a combination of volumes of different heights and inclinations. A green roof was used to enhance the building's integration into its environment.

142-143 bottom The prospects reveal forms close to those of the local vernacular architecture. A series of differently sloping layers allows natural light to enter even the deepest parts of the house.

into the deepest sections of the dwelling. The walls were realized in reinforced cement, left bare in the interior, except in certain cases where they were painted white to emphasize the effect of the natural light. Local basalt covers the floors with a succession of hexagonal slabs. The interiors also include elements of oak treated with oil, which characterize a majority of the coatings for ceilings, enhanced at certain points with steel detailing. The kitchen and bathroom are distinguished by their marble coatings.

The design of the shell was conceived so as to exploit the passive gains necessary to offset the extreme climatic conditions of the Skagafjördur fjord. Ample windows were thus planned, allowing for capture of the sun's heat and, at the same time, appreciation of the views of the cliffs on the islands opposite, and of the nearby hills. The shell is well isolated by means of the green roof and the thick, reinforced cement walls, coated on the outside with untreated cedar elements, destined to change color with the passing of the seasons. Heat is provided by a radiant floor installation integrated by a series of radiators, both powered by a geothermal installation that also provides sanitary hot water and meets part of the electrical energy requirement. A hydroelectric installation provides the remainder of the electricity requirement in case of need.   B.S.

144 A corner of the living room reveals the function of the large windows: full enjoyment of the uncontaminated natural landscape surrounding the dwelling.

144-145 The interiors play upon tones of gray, with the reinforced cement left bare and the basalt flooring realized using stones excavated on-site to make way for the foundations. The ceiling and furnishings of wood provide visual warmth.

Maison Passive 95

BESSANCOURT, FRANCE

This passive house is located in the center of a village northwest of Paris, meshed with an urban fabric characterized by a dense interweave of little streets, courtyards, and small buildings. The quest for the greatest possible energy efficiency started with the correct orientation of thebuilding, which required closing the north side almost completely to the exterior so as to keep heat loss occurring prevalently on the north side – to a minimum. This is opposed by the south prospect, completely transparent and facing the garden so as to best exploit the heat of the sun in winter.

The first certified passive house in the region of Ile-de-France, this dwelling in Bessancourt is considered the most energy-efficient residence in France. More than just an exercise in ecological planning and construction, the dwelling designed by Karawitz Architecture also provides a high quality of living for its occupants. "Aesthetically, it is a sculptural and abstract replica of the traditional house," the architects explain.

The entire shell is covered by an uninterrupted succession of untreated bamboo elements, destined to gray over time, similar in appearance to that large sort of house typical of the vernacular architecture of this part of the Ile-de-France. On the south side, the bamboo elements were assembled on a series of metallic frames that slide on horizontal tracks, to create a series of window shutters that can be completely opened to make this side entirely transparent. Centered on this side, a metal balcony has been fashioned the function of extending to extend the interior rooms on both floors toward a hybrid space with a particular aesthetic. Once closed, the bamboo skin shades the glass-paneled front, playing with light, and serving also to conserve heat on cold nights and to screen the sun in summer, preventing the interior spaces from overheating.

The distribution of interior space was determined on the basis of bioclimatic exposure. For this reason, the building was divided into two parallel sections: the first, deeper and exposed to the south, hosts the main living quarters; the narrower section toward the north includes the sanitary facilities and the stairway connecting the two levels. These segments are separated into a structural spine composed of X-lam (crosswise laminated plywood) panels, left partly open to connect these two different sections; the rest was closed to fashion a space for the installations, some wall closets, and the kitchen fixtures. The conduits for the forced ventilation installation – absolutely necessary in realizing a passive house – are left partly visible, as are the simple fluorescent tubesused for much of the lighting. These tubes are powered mostly by the photovoltaic installation on the south layer of the cover, which produces about 3200 kWh of electrical energy every year.

The house was built entirely with natural materials, primarily of local origin, and even in the interiors, to the extent possible, they have been left visible and untreated. A platform foundation of reinforced cement concrete, appropriately insulated, supports the building structure, made of solid wooden panels in crosswise layers, and insulated with cellulose padding and wood fiber panels, so as to bring the entire shell to the level of transmittance values typical of passive houses.   B.S.

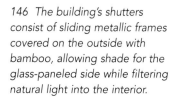

146 The building's shutters consist of sliding metallic frames covered on the outside with bamboo, allowing shade for the glass-paneled side while filtering natural light into the interior.

146-147 The south prospect presents a façade composed entirely of a series of shutters. Once opened, they reveal a transparent membrane equipped with a balcony on the first level.

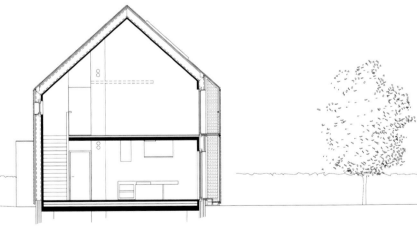

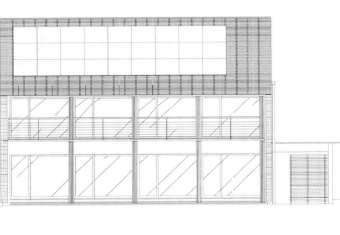

147 bottom Prospects and
sections demonstrate how the
project fully respects the rules
of bioclimatics. The transparency
of the south side, onto which
the principal rooms face, is offset
by the closure of the north side,
which borders the service
facilities.

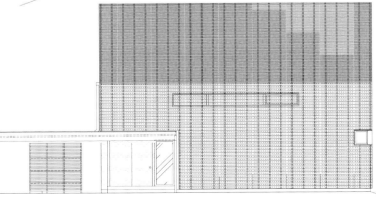

148 The corridor for accessing the various first-floor rooms, facing toward the north, reveals the central structural spine composed of panels of laminated wood.

148-149 *The living room and kitchen occupy most of the ground floor and reveal the structural part of the building in laminated wood, left unfinished.*

Salvaging a *tabià*

SELVA DI CADORE, ITALY

The transformation of this barn, realized by studio EXiT architetti associati (Francesco Loschi, Giuseppe Pagano, and Paolo Panetto) of Treviso, tells much about how the Alpine regions are changing. Even though beset by many contradictions, regions like Voralberg and later Tyrol in Austria, and Alto Adige in Italy, not to mention parts of Switzerland, have become case studies on an international level for implementing policies favoring development that does not damage the principal resource for local economies: the Alpine environment, as extraordinary as it is delicate.

Selva di Cadore is a municipality nestled in one of the areas of the Veneto Dolomites having the greatest scenic – and therefore touristic – value. The conversion of a barn into a dwelling is not unusual. But EXiT's refined project highlights a completely changed attitude regarding the heritage of traditional constructions. There is a great awareness of how much spontaneous architecture, even poor examples such as stalls and haylofts (such was the function of the *tabià*), can teach in terms of the limited resources available and the environmental characteristics of sites. In this case, the wooden portion of the existing structure was disassembled, and the structure, which contained a stone basement, in accordance with tradition, was freed of the incongruous additions that had stratified through the years. Much of the wooden material of the original building, carefully identified, even in terms of the systems for joining, was then put back to use and integrated with other recovered timber to maintain the homogeneous appearance of the shell.

The original bearing structure of wood was integrated into a new structure of steel, left, for the most part, visible in the interiors and, in certain cases, covered with wood.

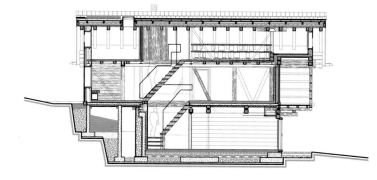

150 top Larch shingles and photovoltaic modules: on the roof of the tabià, local constructional tradition meets sustainable innovation.

150 bottom From the old stable-hayloft, three inhabitable floors have been fashioned, and even the volume beneath the roof has been recovered for use.

150-151 The material with which the tabià was constructed has been recovered and put to use again. The exterior thus reveals little of the radical nature of the intervention performed upon this building.

151 bottom The structure of the original building has been respected: the wooden structure of the upper floors rests upon the stone foundation.

EXIT ARCHITETTI
ASSOCIATI

152 top The recovery of the space beneath the roof allowed for fashioning an inhabitable space.

152 bottom The building was equipped with a new steel structure, which integrates effectively with the wooden elements.

152-153 The stube that dominates the day zone contributes to the building's self-sufficiency in terms of energy. The photovoltaic modules provide enough energy to satisfy electrical and thermal requirements.

Fir and larch were the two types of wood used: the first for plugging, the second for structural parts and coating the exterior. The larch utilized for the exteriors is a naturally resistant wood that ages elegantly, taking on grayish tones, needing no chemical treatments. The renewal of the building thus does not erase the memory of the pre-existing and, indeed, it even enhances the value of the interiors, where the use of few materials – wood (again, larch or fir), local stone, steel, and white plaster – respects the essential character of this architecture, combining frugality with extreme elegance.

The attention of the architects toward the signs of time,

even when minimal, can be found in every detail. Bearing traces of the flow of time demonstrates the durability of an architectural work, and its relation to the function for which it was originally conceived.

A true symbol of this new rapport between tradition and innovation is the roof, where the mantle of larch shingles coexists with a photovoltaic installation integrated into the layer. From the point of view of energy, the house is thus nearly self-sufficient, since the energy produced by the photovoltaic modules satisfies not only the electrical requirements but also the thermal. To these the *stube* also

contributes; situated in the large living room on the first floor, it hosts also the kitchen, bedroom and bathrooms. On the ground floor, enclosed by the stone basement, are two more bedrooms and their accompanying bathrooms.

The Alpine regions are surpassing in a brilliant manner their past of marginality and of somewhat episodic development, taking on an unexpected role as cultural point of reference on a European level. A historic reversal between mountainous tracts and plain areas, in which architecture and the culture of architects are among the primary driving factors.   M.M.

Little Rock Prefab

LITTLE ROCK, USA

A group of architecture students designed and built this living module under the guidance of Michael Hughes, associate professor in the architecture department at the University of Arkansas during the time of the project. The project was part of the university's Design-Build program, which seeks to give architecture students an experience that combines art, craft, civic outreach, and social responsibility. Its goal was a new type of prefab living structure, both ecological and economical; it was carried out in collaboration with professionals, entrepreneurs, and a nonprofit association dedicated to revitalizing local communities. They worked to transform the mobile home, a type of low-income housing widespread in both urban and rural America since the 1950s, in response to habitational emergencies among the most disadvantaged social categories has implied from a bare-essentials dwelling into a real home one would want to live in.

This reinterpretationhas been reinterpreted, seeking to improve it in qualitative and aesthetic improvement, combined traditional and innovative construction techniques. It employedand employing ecological materials and strategies that favor energy savings and passive techniques, so as to respond, at the same time, to the local culture and climatic conditions. The risk of overheating the interior was reduced with making use of sizable overhangs, translucent glass panes, window shutters, and green elements providing shade, combined with cross ventilation and natural lighting. The luminosity of the interiors is ensured by an open planimetric arrangement and by attention to details directed at improving the quality even the very idea of an economical dwelling.

Interior and exterior surfaces were integrated, replacing cramped quarters this with a more spacious design. The main

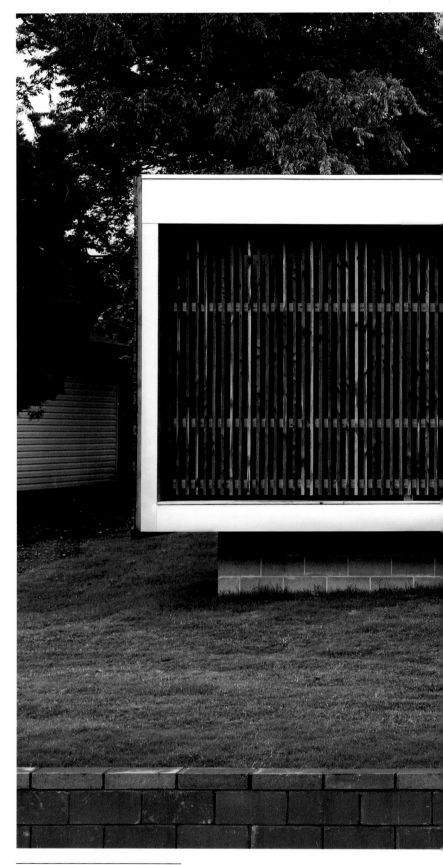

154 top The cleft in the exterior covering allows a view of the street from a private courtyard structured as an open-air room, through a window that can close to provide privacy for the occupants.

154-155 top The principal façade includes the entryway and is furnished with a portico that serves as a semipublic space.

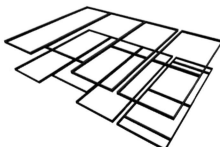

154-155 bottom The structural axonometry reveals that the building uses the balloon frame constructional system, which allows for realizing buildings of prefabricated wood with a high degree of project flexibility.

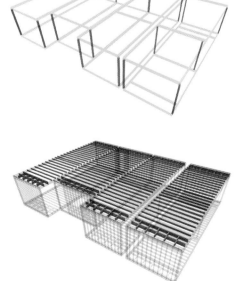
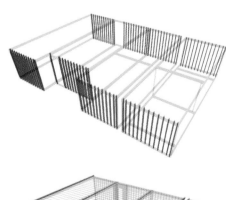
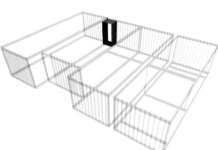

interior space includes a living room, kitchen, and dining area, with an open plan of about 7 x 13 m (about 23' x 43'), and is projected toward a series of exterior spaces aimed at improving the quality of the residents' daily life. Apresence of a succession of porticos, more or less visible from the street, as well as a courtyard and a patio at the back of the dwelling, encourage meeting one's neighbors in a semipublic space and cultivating new social relationships.

The entire dwelling measures little more than 110 sq m (about 1180 sq ft), but these project strategies, together with attention to detail and the presence of a bathroom interpreted

as a small wellness center, make it seem more spacious. The light-colored surfaces dilate the sense of space and optimize the diffusion of natural light. The wooden interior dividing walls eliminate the need to frame the doors, which are not recognizable when they are closed. The entire dwelling is composed of three prefab modules, integrated with that of the portico. Eighty percent of the building – including cover, doors, windows, installations, and a good part of the coatings – was assembled in a warehouse. Practically speaking, the only things realized on-site were the foundations and the connections between modules, along with a few finishing touches.   B.S.

---

156 top The transparent wall of the day zone allows a full view of the street and invites light to enter.

156 bottom The day zone includes an open-view kitchen, the furnishings for which are, for the most part, integrated into the structure of the building

because they depend on the position of the prefabricated elements.

157 This zone unfolds to the entry portico by means of a transparent wall allowing various systems of opening, for natural interior ventilation in various sorts of weather.

werner tscholl architekt (casa ri[
(residência em tijucopava) - pietro carmir
& jeremy till (9/10 stock orchard street
(g-box) - olavi koponen (house kotilo)
van leeuwen (beukenburg) - davide n
fujimoto architects (final wooden hou
muros) - mareines+patalano arquit
village house).

the poetry of natural materials

i) - marcos acayaba arquitetos

e *(casa in pietra)* - sarah wigglesworth

- sarah wigglesworth architects

architectuurbureau sluijmer en

acullo architects *(house in ticino)* - sou

e) - al borde arquitectos *(casa entre*

tura *(casa folha)* - mxarchitecture *(1M*

the poetry of natural materials

Architecture is one of the disciplines by means of which we have attempted – especially throughout the last century – to exploit, modify, and artificially force as much as possible the materials and forms of energy that nature makes available to us, to satisfy our own desires, those of the developed world. Humanity's excessive impact on the landscape, with countless outsized works of architecture completely extraneous to the context in which they are situated, is the result of this widespread attitude, which continues in spite of the fact that nature us, on every occasion,continually reminds us that we are part of her and that because of this we must respect her.

The poetics of architecture can be seen in those features of buildings that satisfy our profoundest desires, those that connect with our concept of harmony connected with and our true essence as beings who only in nature can find an empathetic and immediate response to our primary needs. The solutions that nature herself adopts to ensure life on our planet still amaze us, and continue to be a source of inspiration for research and projects in every discipline.

The architecture of the past not been removed from this fascination, recallingevoked nature's proportions and solutions to allow realizing environments to realize structures that can protect people from bad weather, or celebrate the greatness of nature and of God. In recent years we have witnessed some attempts at recapturing the close connection between nature and architecture, thanks to a certain number of architects who are based on returning to nature as a point of reference for their projects, while technological equipmentavailing themselves of technology that up until a few decades ago was unimaginable.

is the use of These environmentally conscious architects use natural materials, of local origin if possible, which are to be displayed for what they are, without concealing them, and respecting their nature, employing each of them according to its proper potential, and exalting their aesthetic qualities through equally natural finishes. The result is a feeling of welcome and familiarity that recalls the principal values of domestic architecture. An exemplary building in this sense is the Final Wooden House (or Next Generation House), the dwelling planned by the studio Fujimoto Architects, situated on the bank of the River Kuma at Kumamura in Japan. Here wood shows itself to be a natural material capable of projecting itself into the future (not by chance, the name of the project alludes to the next generation). Owing to a wise play of volumes, it defines the external shell, the interior coverings, and the minimal furnishings one needs in a house. A second example is the Casa Entre Muros by albordE in Ecuador, which owes its form to a succession of seven bearing elements realized in tamped raw earth recovered from the excavation out of which the building rises. In this example, the palette of materials expands to stone and wood, utilized in honest ways without decorative finishes to exalt their characteristics and aesthetics.

The prerogatives of natural materials can be underscored even more profoundly by taking inspiration from nature in the design of architectural works themselves. In this case, we are speaking of organic architecture, a genre that includes all the buildings based on references to forms from nature, never linear, and responding to specific proportions for their harmonic appearance. This project attitude animates the affinity between man and nature, develops, building, much like primitive architecture, from the inside out, ensuring protection and at the same time, openness. The organic buildings are constructed using simple materials and delineating forms and structures typical of nature, such as spirals and fractals, the basis of revealing the laws by which organisms grow and natural forces like sun, wind and water appear. *The Kotilo House by Finnish architect Olavi Koponen responds fully to these requirements, enclosing within a wooden spiral all habitational functions, in a continuous succession of spaces that, though lacking interior partitions, provides intimacy, a welcoming atmosphere, and comfort. A second example, constructed on the other side of the world in Brazil, the Casa Fohla designed by Ivo Mareines and Rafael Patalano, demonstrates that this inspiration drawing upon references to nature is universal. These two architectural works, while differing in their appearance (partly in response to opposite climatic requirements), have in common their reference to the spiral, the fluidity of their interior spaces, and their nearly exclusive use of wood. The second project owes its name to the particular design of the cover, composed of a series of leaves, under which the adjustable glass-paneled walls seek maximum openness toward and integration with nature. The use of natural materials helps quite a bit to satisfy this aspiration, as demonstrated by the House in Ticino by Davide Macullo, sided with a skin of copper conceived to allow appreciation of the surrounding landscape, and the modern stone donjon of the Rizzi home by Werner Tscholl. Both of these dwellings are integrated into slopes, to respecting their natural profile and safeguarding the visual equilibrium of the environment in which they are immersed – confirming the rule according to which a building must belong to the landscape and not be imposed upon it. The same principle inspired architect Pietro Carmine in the construction of his house at Cannero on Lake Maggiore, a dwelling that integrates with the natural landscape and the buildings of the village to which it belongs. The key to this project is not only respect for the environment, but also the use of exclusively natural materials and, above all, local*

vernacular construction techniques, showcased by inserting certain innovative elements. Traditional architects and builders have taken centuries to explore all the potential and expressiveness of locally available materials. And this heritage of knowledge can be exploited by today's project planners in realizing contemporary architectural works that respect the history of the place and the landscape. This is the case for the 1M Village House, a project by mXarchitecture realized on one of the islands of the Cyclades in spite of the severe protective regulations regarding the landscape. Adopting traditional constructional techniques and local materials permitted an optimum bioclimatic result.

Natural materials can even be inflected using contemporary architectural language in a style that seeks to both transcend and respect the traditional relationship between form and function. One example is the house at Tijucopava by Marcos Acayaba, presenting the linear features of contemporary architecture organized into a structure whose design was inspired partly by the trees of the Brazilian forest surrounding it. In Europe, we find the Beukenburg residence, realized at Utrecht by Architectuurbureau Sluijmer en van Leeuwen. It sits in the middle of protected woodland completely visible from the dwelling through a shell covered mostly with glass, enriched by the presence of wood and copper so as to recall the features of contemporary Dutch architecture. An interesting example in this sense is the house-studio of Sarah Wigglesworth realized in London by Wigglesworthherself and Jeremy Till. The architect was able to experiment in her own home with various natural materials in a syntax of traditional and innovative techniques, combining wood, cellulose, hay, lime, and sand with discards from demolitions, cement, steel sheet, and polycarbonate slabs, obtaining an unusual and profoundly contemporary language. B.S.

Casa Rizzi

SAN MARTINO AL MONTE, ITALY

A castle to live in was the dream the commissioner presented to Werner Tscholl, who designed him a tower, at 1740 m (5708 ft), dominating Val Martello and Val Venosta. The characterizing the construction materials – natural stone, chestnut wood, and white marble from Lasa – were borrowed from castles in the environs, which the architect himself had restored.

The insertion of contemporary elements, such as transparent walls and metallic frameworks, permits the structure to open toward the enchanting panorama of the valley and allows natural light to enter the interior even on winter days when the sun is low on the horizon. For illumination, a transparent cylinder was designed and outfitted with a mesh of terraces, balconies, and observation points. From this glass-paneled structure, the light enters, even transversely, so as to illuminate all the spaces, passively producing heat, which in turn is accumulated by the considerable mass of the external stone shell, with its back to the slope and closed toward the street. The keep, about 22 m (72 ft) high, is accessed by an actual drawbridge made of steel and electronically activated, leading to the highest level of the dwelling; hosts the bedrooms occupy the lower floor. To reach the living room, the heart of the house, facing onto a wooden terrace seemingly suspended above the valley, we need to descend one more level, through the central staircase; as the outsidethe garden can be accessed from the lowest floor. For the lowest level, the commissioner requested a bona fide

162 top The residence is equipped with a garden that includes a small reflecting pool, concealed from public view by the natural slope of the terrain.

162-163 The inside of the modern stone keep was emptied so as to bring sunlight and heat into the residence, as well as to showcase the view of the underlying valley.

163 bottom The strategic position of the building required careful planning to ensure maximum integration with the surrounding landscape, both constructed and natural.

164-165 The hollow section of the center of the tower, delimited by transparent walls, is equipped with a glass-paned cover that allows natural light to penetrate deeply.

165 top The stone cylinder characterizing the residence holds a dominant position over the valley, allowing full appreciation of the splendid Alpine panorama.

oasis of well-being for body and soul. Inspired by Alpine lakes and meditation gardens, the architect designed a swimming pool with a green-blue bottom, surrounded by hydro-massage equipment, saunas, and bars, enclosed by circular stone-covered walls, open at certain strategic points to ensure that from here, as well, the marvelous views will nourish the spirit.

The stone walls of the external shell present a nucleus of reinforced cement, whereas the horizontal structures, except the first, cast in white cement, are realized with wooden floors using the Brettstapelbau technique, by which massive planks of seasoned red fir are placed together, coupled, and nailed, so as to produce a solid bearing element. The interior partitions are structured with dry-mounted wood frames, covered with wood paneling or lime plastering, while the floors are covered with solid wood planks treated with oil and natural wax, to contrast the "coldness" of the stone. The furnishing elements are essential and noninvasive, and cabinets in solid wood are arranged to create a minimalist but welcoming space. Illuminating bodies are Lighting is incorporated into the furnishings and into the internal shell so the artificial lights become an architectural element on the level of what was done for the natural component.   B.S.

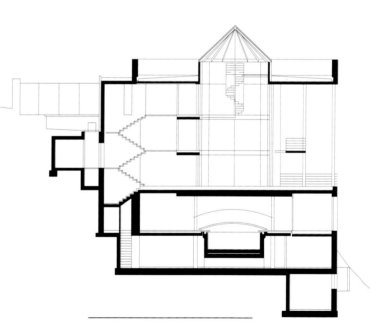

165 bottom This section shows how the building is partly supported on the mountain, with its access from the street on the highest floor, thus ensuring maximum privacy for the inhabitants.

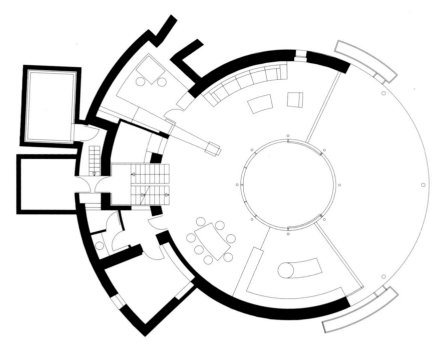

166 center right The hollow cylinder fashioned from the center terminates at the living room, where it resolves into a small greenhouse where one can relax appreciating the sun's warmth and the splendid view.

166 bottom and 166-167 The swimming pool occupies a good part of the next-to-last level, introduced into an environment where the coatings alternate between wood and stone. It is outfitted with a terrace that opens onto the underlying panorama.

166 top The plan shows the development of the building's living room, which is organized as an open space outfitted with some service quarters. It extends toward the exterior with a large terrace.

166 center left The living room is embellished with a modern steel chimney for burning wood, which visually separates the dining area from the conversation nook.

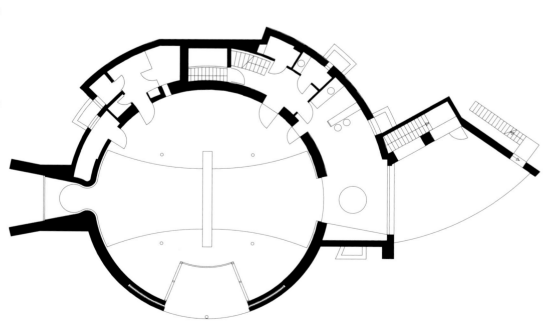

168-169 The house is completely immersed in the exuberant vegetation of the Mata Atlântica, the rain forest covering a good part of the coast of Brazil.

Residência em Tijucopava
GUARUJÁ, BRAZIL

The houses designed by Marcos Acayaba in the 1990s – starting with the residence conceived in 1990 for Hélio Olga de Souza Jr. and continuing with the Residência Ricardo Dias Baeta at Iporanga in 1991 and the home designed for his own family in 1997 – call attention to the merits of the new Brazilian wooden architecture.

The idea of building with wood still is often criticized due to a misunderstanding about the meaning of attention for the environment. Construction that requires felling trees, when considered superficially, does not seem to be the best option in terms of ecology. In a country like Brazil, where conservation of the environment, particularly the forests, can create challenges of dramatic dimensions, killing trees seems especially irresponsible.

In the 1990s, the collaboration between Acayaba and ITA Construtora di Hélio Olga de Souza Jr. produced prototypes of ecological wooden architecture and developed a school. The Acayaba house is its most mature example. The context is the coastal band covered with virgin forest, the Mata Atlântica, where the terrain suitable for building is often steeply sloped. In order to avoid excavating land and, inevitably, felling trees, Acayaba elaborated a spectacular construction model that succeeds in drawing out the best characteristics of the site while minimizing the modifications required for new construction.

From its plan view, the house is a succession of floors of irregular, hexagonal form, with sides that extend to constitute a prow, almost, protruding from the vegetation toward the

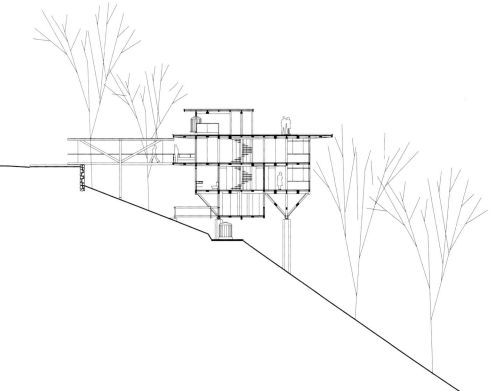

169 bottom The impact of the construction upon the terrain is minimal, since the building plan calls for only three support points.

170 bottom A covered
footbridge connects the house
to the street, leading directly
to the day zone level hosting
the kitchen, dining room, living
room, and two covered terraces.

landscape. The plan, which allows access to the best panoramic view of the ocean, was conceived, above all, to respect the natural condition of the terrain, reducing the support points to just three.

From three plinths of reinforced cement, the structure rises to four full stories (one small additional floor is hung from the loft of the lowest floor). All the structural parts are realized in wood, prefabricated in the workshop and mounted according to a triangular geometry, plugged with concrete tiles, lightened in the cover lofts.

On the façade, the geometry of the plan comes alive in an articulation of balconies and terraces emphasizing the search for interpenetration between interior and exterior. The actual roof-terrace extends more than 2 m (more than 2 yd) beyond the façade beneath, protecting it effectively from the frequent and powerful tropical downpours.

On the main floor, and connected to the street by a bridge covered with wood, is a large continuous space comprising the kitchen and living room, with three terraces. On the intermediate floor is the night zone, with three bedrooms and accompanying bathrooms. The bottom floor hosts the laundry room and the maid's quarters. The four stories are connected by a wooden spiral staircase. The interior dividing walls are made of plywood panels.

Owing to the particular structural pattern, the entire construction was realized through the assembly of light, small pieces. This process avoided the use of heavy and cumbersome construction equipment that would have aggravated the impact on the terrain. In this manner, the house was assembled in just four months by only four workmen. M.M.

170-171 The two upper floors of the dwelling (terrace and day zone) emerge from the forest, allowing the residents to appreciate the view of the surrounding landscape.

171 bottom The two lower floors host the night zone; the bottom one is for service quarters. This last floor is suspended from the structure of the floor top.

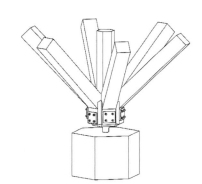

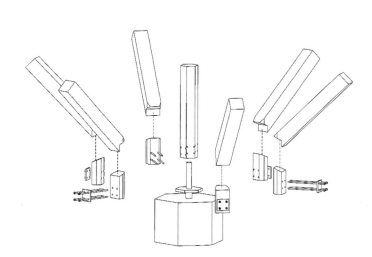

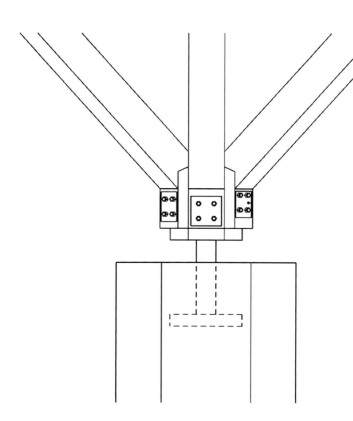

172 top and center The assembly schema for one of the three support elements shows how the wooden "branches" fork off from the reinforced cement "trunk."

172 bottom The inspiration from nature for this detail is obvious. The project planner has also used it in other realizations in situations similar to the one illustrated here.

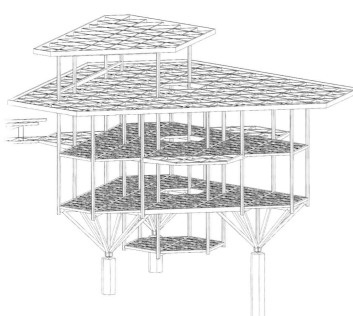

172-173 The lowest level of the dwelling is equipped with an independent access via a wooden bridge, seen to the left.

173 bottom The various stories have the form of an irregular hexagon whose surface is subdivided into a dense triangular mesh.

174 top, center and bottom The dimensions of hexagons gradually decrease in correspondence with descending height. At the center of each floor the spiral stairway connects the various interior spaces.

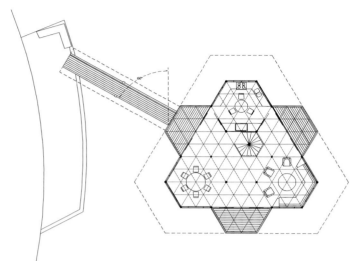

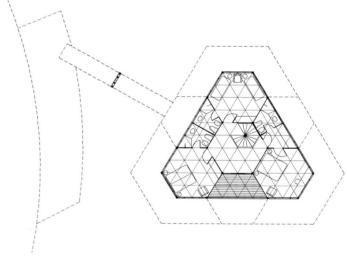

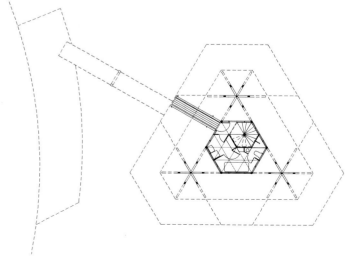

174-175 The kitchen occupies the north corner of the day zone. Here, as well, the dominant material is wood.

175 bottom The day zone is organized as a broad single space, totally open to the surrounding nature.

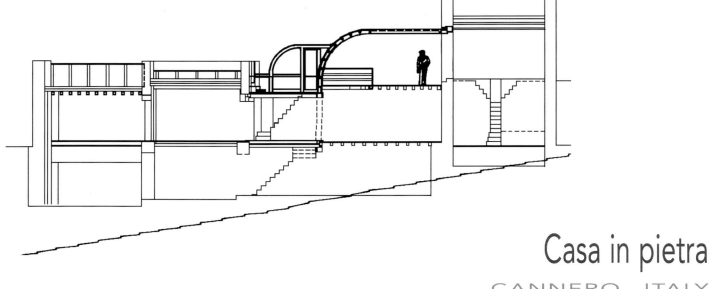

Casa in pietra
CANNERO, ITALY

Active during the years when the culture of the bio-ecological project was beginning to penetrate even into Italy, Milanese architect Pietro Carmine – recently deceased – realized in his home at Cannero, the locality on Lake Maggiorefrom where he was born, the consummation of the project planning principles he posited as the foundation of his work. Today the term "holistic" can appear a bit dated, but in fact, the inclusion of social, environmental, cultural, and economic criteria in project planning is still what distinguishes a completely "sustainable" building. It means evaluating a very broad set of variables allowing comparison between the positive and negative aspects connected with the construction of the building, not only in the short term, but also in the long run. It is an approach that today appears a bit outmoded, if only regarding respect of the evidence presented on energy-related aspects.

The house at Cannero, completed in 2000, contains many elements of great interest from various points of view: use of natural and local materials, innovation and revitalization of constructional know-how, application of bioclimatic strategies, and introduction into the landscape. The latter is perhaps the aspect that appears with greatest emphasis: the external shell resumes with extraordinary precision the dry-mounted structure of the stone retaining walls that support and define the terracing that characterizes this part of the lake shore. An imitation mimesis that at the same time shows an appreciation of the traditional manner of construction. Viewed from the lake, the volume of the house practically dissolves into the succession of levels of dry-mounted walls. Only the large curved window fixture of the solar greenhouse stands out, covering a part of the dining room. The structure of the dwelling planimetry appears clearly to be modeled on the terracing from which it arises; the form is irregular, squeezed between the slope and the alley that rises uphill from the lakeshore. The building develops in length and height. Parts of the rocky ground were incorporated into the construction and emerge in the interiors, for example, in the first floor sitting room, as a further emphasis of the building's roots in the terrain of the construction to the territory. In the realization of the masonry shell, as well as in other details, the desire to appreciate local materials – and the traditional artisanal techniques that make best use of them – emerges visibly that best know how to make use of these materials. The house demonstrates the architect's openness to innovation, such as using bamboo (the local variety *Phyllostachys viridis mitis*, which can reach heights of 18 m (about 60 ft) to "reinforce" the vault in pozzolanic cement covering the spaces originally destined for study and archives. Externally, stonethat assumes the role of protagonist in determining the appearance of the building, whether elaborated in the dry mounted walls or put to use in large monolithic elements.

But it is not only the attention to "kilometer zero" that guided the project planning choices: wholesomeness of interior climate, absence of harmful emissions from substances present in constructional or finishing materials, and attentively excluding materials that might represent a risk to the health of the craftsman (excepting the normal dangers of a construction site) were important criteria. Some of the interior walls were realized using the wattle-and-daub technique (a mixture of earth and straw on a base of willow branches framed within a structure of chestnut wood), or with an insulating mixture of earth and straw. Finally, many of the materials utilized were recovered directly on-site from the demolition of pre-existing constructions. All of this makes the house at Cannero a prime a demonstrative example of what it means to apply a holistic approach to an architectural project.   M.M.

---

176 *The building rises on a long narrow lot and develops parallel to the alley that provides access to the property.*

177 *The attention placed on using constructional techniques and materials from local tradition produces results that integrate perfectly with the landscape.*

178 The greenhouse encloses the dining room. Besides functioning as a passive apparatus for heating, it allows for full appreciation of the lake.

179 top The rocky slope "enters" into the house, as it does into the living room, where the rough surface of the boulder contrasts with the soft forms of the surfaces plastered with clay.

179 bottom In the hot season, the glass paneling of the greenhouse can be completely opened, facilitating natural ventilation and preventing overheating of the interior.

9/10 Stock Orchard Street

LONDON, UNITED KINGDOM

Sarah Wigglesworth's house-studio in Islington, an urban district north of the City of London, is a sort of manifesto. At the same time, it is a place to experiment with materials and sustainable technologies. "Better to have too many ideas than not to have any at all," the studio architects at 9-10 Stock Orchard Street declare in presenting their project philosophy. And this architectural complex displays a truly surprising quantity of ideas put into practice.

The project's three sectionsis articulated – two dedicated to living spaces, one to office space – rise from a plot of land bordering a railway line in a densely built residential zone. Situated at the end of a dead-end street characterized by the classic row houses of greater London, the building stands out with its façade covered with synthetic material like that of a down windbreaker jacket.

And this is only the beginning of the journey, an adventure of applying the most unusual materials of *green building*, where the matching, only apparently casual, of volumes and surfaces conceals a project that is highly attentive to every detail.

The volume in most direct contact with the railway noise is the one containing the studio, resting on a series of pillars constructed using a "gabionade" system of recycling discards from the demolition of cement works. But it is on the upper floor that the most daring experiments begin: the wall facing the railway line is realized using wooden framing filled with sacks of sand, cement, and lime, ensuring optimal thermal and acoustic insulation. The façade near the garden is, again, of wood, but with cellulose insulation. The remaining part of the "L" contains a combined home-office space (the dining room can be used, if necessary, for meetings), followed by the day zone and the night zone. Here the shell is , again, using another wooden structure, but this filling is of one is filled with bales of hay, a material that combines wholesomeness with optimal thermal-acoustic performance. The interior walls are finished with a lime plaster, while the exterior walls are protected by corrugated sheets of galvanized steel or transparent polycarbonate, allowing a view of the wall's composition.

In 2001, when construction was completed, it was perhaps the first time that materials like sandbags or bales of hay had been utilized in an urban context.

While the structure containing the night zone is entirely realized using this technology, the day zone is equipped with a façade almost entirely of glass, with a view of the garden. And to call it a garden is an understatement: a vegetable garden has been fashioned from the green area; a small basin is also planned for purification of gray waters. The vegetation is luxuriant and not limited to the garden: the roof, as well,

180 bottom   The building, situated at the end of a cul-de-sac amid the row houses and the railway, announces itself with curiously "outsized" elements. The side toward the railway has a wooden framing and a filling of sacks of sand, cement, and lime: optimal thermoacoustic insulation, trifling costs.

180-181   Building her own home-studio represented a once-in-a-lifetime opportunity for the project planner to experiment, as in this wall made of bales of hay covered with opaque and transparent corrugated slabs.

is a veritable meadow, with strawberry plants. Another distinctive element rises from the roof: the tower-library, which also enhances the chimney effect activating the natural ventilation of the internal spaces.

Stock Orchard 9-10 is the result of a complex project plan, effected by aiming constantly functionality and frugality of for functional, frugal solutions: clean materials at low cost, simple building techniques, and minimal recourse to installation superstructures. A project in which architecture is the protagonist.

Revitalizing the urban space was one among the many significant outcomes architects Wigglesworth and Till desired for this project: taking the office down to the end of a dead-end street, right in the middle of an exclusively residential area, , as can contribute, as often happens, to a process of requalification, calling other sorts of structures to settle in the neighborhood. And ensuring the presence of a functional and social mix is a key strategy in every project of urban sustainability.   M.M.

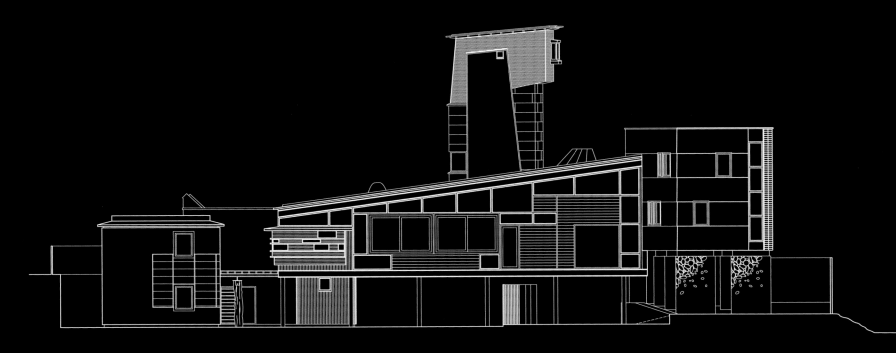

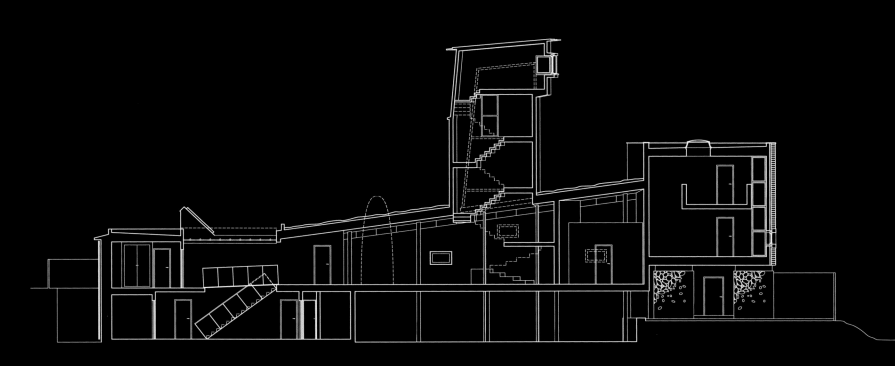

182 top The more electic prospect faces onto the inner courtyard, where surfaces of wood, glass, opaque and transparent corrugated steel, and synthetic fabric alternate.

182 bottom The large ventilation tower, habitable and used for the library, is perhaps the most characteristic element of the entire project.

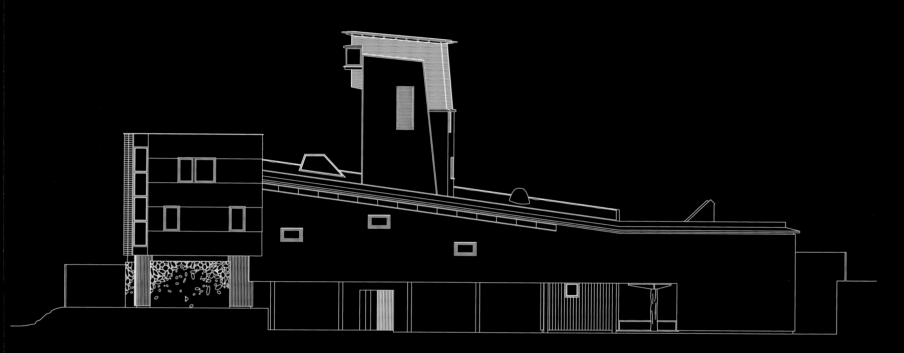

183 top The large inclined cover is, in reality, a green roof, where an attempt was even made to grow strawberries.

183 bottom As revealed in the transverse section of the complex, an ample green area was fashioned on the lot, used also as a phyto-purification basin for gray waters.

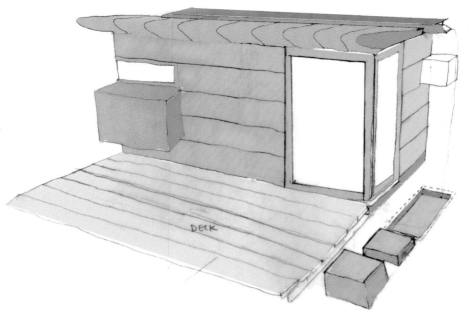

G-Box

LONDON, UNITED KINGDOM

SARAH WIGGLESWORTH ARCHITECTS

The theme of the dwelling in an urban context is often confronted with requirements for expansion, deriving from the evolution of the needs of people during the course of their life and conditioned by numerous constraints, among which are little available space, limited economic resources, difficulty of obtaining permits, and—not last—the need for integration with what has already been constructed. The Sarah Wigglesworth Architects studio has faced these questions by conceiving of a prototype for a prefabricated wooden construction made up of one single room. The project planners' intention was to realize a structure that would be pleasant from an aesthetic point of view, economic, and simple to assemble, thus making it versatile also from the point of view of its possible location, which could be independent or directly connected with an existing structure.

A few months after the definition of the project, called G-Box, the occasion for making it into a concrete realization arrived, a sign that this type of requirement was very widespread, especially in a city like London. One client expressed the need for constructing a small independent structure, in the garden of his row house, where he would be able to perform his work as a graphic designer without having to go very far from home. The building needed to display contemporary features even while being inserted into a context with historical-architectural regulation because of the exclusive presence of residential row houses from the late Victorian era. The G-Box prototype proved to be an adequate response to these requirements, both in form and dimensions, which correspond more or less to those of an individual office. It was well received by the client. The project designers worked at "customizing" the project, equipping the structure with a double window-door, defining a corner that opens out onto the garden, a workspace, and a mobile container, the profile of which partly protrudes from the exterior silhouette, characterizing it together with an analogous glass-enclosed volume on the opposite side. The closures and furnishings were provided in the plant, in accordance with the agreed-upon design. The structure was provided in a kit, which included electrical connections and necessary cabling, ready to be connected to the electrical and telephone networks. It was then assembled by two persons for a cost of approximately £35,000 (about $55,500).

The structure can be made as high as 3 m (about 9.8 ft) and consists in a box of plywood, finished with a few other simple natural materials to ensure that the structure will have a pleasant aesthetic impact as well as a thoroughly up-to-date image. It is raised from the ground using steel supports so as to preclude humidity problems and to allow it to adapt to the various conformations of the lot. The supports, in turn, rests upon the cement foundation. The structure is insulated so that it can even be used on the coldest days of the year; it is covered on the exterior with elements in wood and copper. The closures are composed of wooden frames with double pane glass, whereas the interior coatings are of white oak for the floor and birch plywood for the walls and furnishings. B.S.

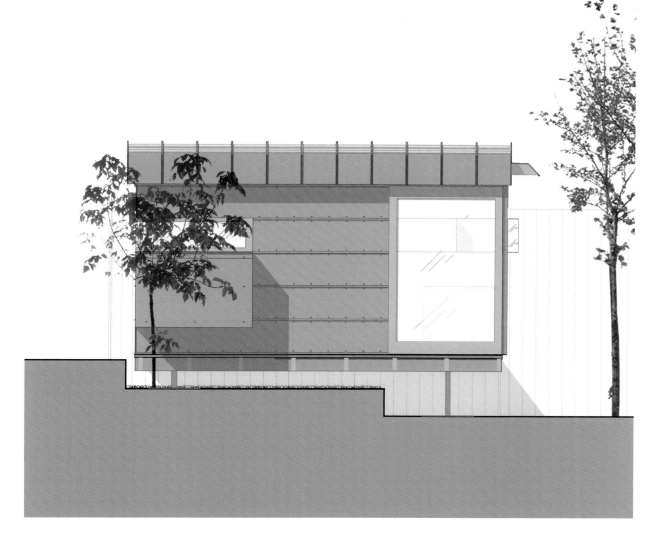

184 top right The aesthetics of the wooden prototype, including the position of the closures, can be varied in accordance with client requirements, concentrating on the combination of three natural materials: wood, copper and glass.

184 bottom left In this case the structure was equipped with an exterior wooden platform and a large door that can be opened to increase the space opening to the exterior during the milder season.

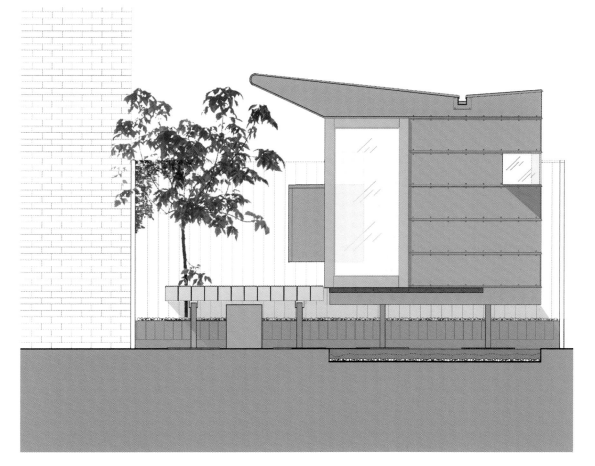

185 top and center The box, consisting of a prefabricated wooden structure, is raised from the ground by a series of metallic supports and a cement foundation.

185 bottom In this case the structure was erected at the bottom of a small garden, complementing a brick row house typical of some London neighborhoods.

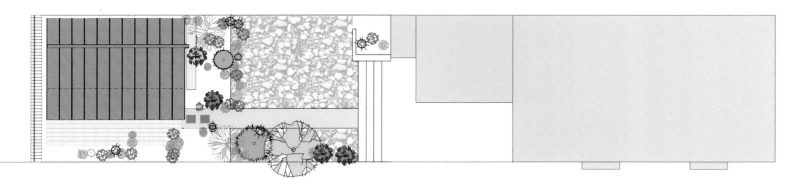

House Kotilo

ESPOO, FINLAND

This particular home was designed as an entry in Asuntomessut (Housing Fair), a competition seeking diverse housing ,destined, for the most part, for young residents of an experimental showcase neighborhood developed in the outskirts of the city of Espoo. On this site, Koponen proposed a single-family residence called Kotilo House (Finnish for seashell house). It was a success, and today the architect himself lives there.

The first inspiration for this project was a model realized by wrapping a piece of plastic around a cylinder, defining an extremely organic form that initially seemed more like a sketch for a sculpture than a point of departure for architecture. The idea took its realized form as a combination of two structures: a "service" parallelepiped ensuring protecting" the residents' privacy, containing a sauna, a small storehouse, and two covered parking places; and a curvilinear volume, wrapped about itself,

186 center left On the access road, the curved volume splits at the first floor, welcoming the natural light that illuminates the night zone and bath area. On the ground floor, the studio opens with a transparent wall decorated in a particular artistic motif.

186 bottom left The building shows its curved silhouette toward the principal street, following its path and revealing its formation from various organically composed segments.

186-187 The dwelling is composed of two distinct structures; the actual residence, characterized by its organic form, is offset by the low volume containing the sauna and the canopy covering the automobile parking spaces.

following the profile of the street. The latter hosts a fluid living space in which the various functions interpenetrate continuously, designed to create a series of spaces suitable for any activity from relaxation to entertaining on festive occasions. , based on their habits, could want to host. The form of the house offers a particular spatial experience, enriched by the effects of the light that penetrates, sometimes unexpectedly, through the openings, changing throughout the day and with the alternating of the seasons.

The distinctive features of this work of architecture are simplicity, intimacy, and naturalness. They are achieved with the use of wood throughout the entire shell, combined with the transparency of the glass, and enriched by the discreet presence of a slender metallic structure and of surfaces in beaten and smoothed cement into which small fragments of colored glass have been embedded. Koponen's declared reference is the vernacular architecture, which succeeds in being welcoming and comfortable through the use of few and simple natural materials, which at the same time introduce the dwelling harmoniously into the landscape.

The particular spiral form is constructed using wooden elements and derives from an intense cooperation between the architect, the structural engineer, and the producer of the building's component elements. It took 6,000 hours to assemble, in spite of which costs did not exceed the average because of effective planning and programming,

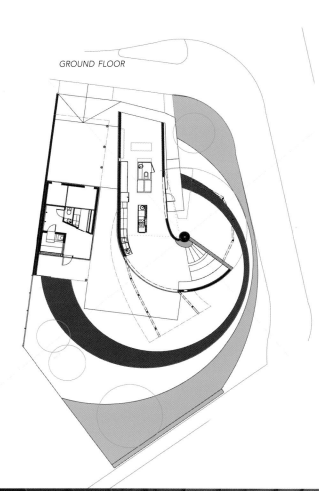

GROUND FLOOR

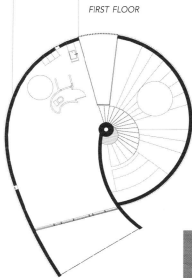

FIRST FLOOR

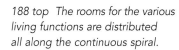

188-189 The living room/dining room zone, heated by the central fireplace and facing onto the outer courtyard through a large glass window, was furnished with a few chairs and a table; the form of the whole matches the proceeding of this part of the building.

188 top The rooms for the various living functions are distributed all along the continuous spiral.

188 bottom A part of the dwelling resolves into a series of steps that rise, with alternate proceeding and different coatings, around the central column.

and the use of simple building techniques. The entire dwelling (walls and floors) is made of prefabricated modules partially supported by a steel structure and twisted about a central column of reinforced cement. The central column also houses a chimney, recalling the domestic hearth.

The exterior surfaces are covered with thick panels of Russian larch and the interior surfaces are covered with thin panels of traditional Finnish poplar. That's a total of 30,000 panels slotted one into another without the need for chemical glues. B.S.

House Kotilo

190 top The large transparent wall of the bathroom faces onto the bedroom area through the transparent split made here to welcome the sunlight. The large window can be screened from the street using a rolling curtain suspended from the ceiling.

190 bottom The shower remains visible, contained in a capsule characterized by an organic form, coated internally in glass paste mosaic; the same element also hosts a section, separated by a door, for the sanitary facilities.

191 The interior and exterior of the building are characterized by a coating of wood shingles, hand placed one by one, with the exception of the floor, which is carpeted on the upper level.

Beukenburg

UTRECHT, THE NETHERLANDS

A house to be built on an estate surrounded by 185 ha (about 460 acres), nestled in a landscape of agricultural and wooded terrains. This is the theme the Utrecht Landscape Foundation proposed in their commission to architects Sluijmer & Van Leeuwen. They welcomed the challenge even while aware of the inherent complexity a project of constructing a new building from scratch amid a pristine landscape.

First of all, along with the commissioners, they carefully selected the building site for the new dwelling that would join the other four already present within the estate. The new house rises from the site of an old, crumbling farmhouse on a clearing in the woods. The fact that it was possible to immerse the building completely in nature inspired the project planners to make the shell as transparent as possible except for the north face, which remains mostly closed for bioclimatic reasons. On this side, the building is characterized by a copper membrane that creates a profile typical of contemporary architecture while also recalling features of the local farm buildings. The materials adopted are natural in origin and among the lightest available, in order to build a house that could be tedintroduced delicately into its context a building with while offering features that are highly decisive, as is traditional in contemporary Dutch architecture.

The side closed in copper, where the entry is located, represents the formal side of the dwelling, which is transparent on the remaining sides owing to its continuous glass shell of glass, screened on the shorter sides to the east and west and partly screened on the principal side to the south. This was done to avoid overheating in summer and also to ensure a bit of privacy for the inhabitants. The screening was created using

192-193 top The house is distributed over two floors and resolved on three sides with a transparent shell, partly screened by a series of wooden fillets that filter the natural light.

192 bottom The copper shell that covers the north face assumes a curvilinear form, gradually transmuting into the

cover and protruding over the south side, providing the shade needed in summer.

192-193 bottom right The transparency of the walls of the house, rising on a flat lot, allows the occupants to appreciate the view of the surrounding park, centuries old and now protected.

ARCHITECTUURBUREAU SLUIJMER EN VAN LEEUWEN

a succession of wooden planks that go in and out in alternating manner from the glass-paneled shell on the southern side, underscoring the natural transition between the home's interior and exterior spaces.

The same south prospect fully reveals the interior distribution of the dwelling, resolved for the most part onto two floors, except for the two sections on the shorter sides, where there are two terraces, one of which is covered by the copper roof. The ground floor is organized according to a free and open distribution of functions, so views of the surrounding landscape and natural lighting can enter every corner of the house. The secret of the simplicity and formal elegance of this project lies in its attention to details, which allowed for very thin walls and floors, in favor of helping to create the sense of lightness that the architects intended, from the very beginning, to transmit. B.S.

---

194 *The living room is located in the east part of the home, where the transparent shell is screened by a series of wooden elements to avoid overheating the interior in summer.*

195 *The rooms on the ground floor are accessed through a double-height corridor oriented toward the north, receiving light from the skylights positioned at the upper part of the roof.*

House in Ticino

GERRA, SWITZERLAND

Constructed on a slope facing the valley between Locarno and Bellinzona, toward Lake Maggiore, a single-family home at Gerra Agarone designed by Lugano architect Davide Macullo attests to the search for a different way of settling on the terrain. Instead of supporting an nth parallelepiped on the gently sloping surface with its perfect exposure – for which reason, already densely built – the volume is superimposed onto the natural profile of the terrain, following it so the cover forms a sort of floor level parallel to the soil, beneath which the living spaces are distributed.

The visual impact of the new volume is thus diminished; the dark color and the lightness of the exterior coating accentuate the mimetic intention.

The house spreads over three levels, two partially underground, with only the top floor completely visible. An entrance "cave" at street level, allows access to the vehicle access and garage; the intermediate story houses the kitchen and service areas; the top level comprises the vast day zone and two bedrooms that extend toward the exterior environment with covered patio and access to the garden and swimming pool.

Once the dwelling was defined, the next step was to to imagine its physical nature, in its relation with the inhabitants, also in regard to sensorial sensory aspects and elements contributing to the well-being of the residents. The goals for this phase of the project were the wholesomeness of interior spaces, energy efficiency, and the use of renewable or recyclable materials. The resulting strategy was based on three materials: cement, wood and copper.

The first two levels, partly wedged into the slope, were realized in reinforced concrete; the top floor is of wood. The basement sunk into the terrain provides climate control while the wood offers wholesomeness and comfort in the day zone where the family spends most of its time. On this level, the construction using prefabricated wooden blocks allowed the shell, structure, and interior partitions to make use of a single system, all with the flexibility to allow for future modification of the interior.

The shell of wooden blocks is protected on the outside by an isolating layer and waterproofing. The most external skin is a coating made of modular elements of copper mesh having the function of for protection and screening.

A high level of recyclability – not only in the system of prefabricated wooden blocks, but also in the copper coating –

is this project's major contribution in terms of sustainability of the construction cycle; which a contribution is made contributing also is the notable reduction of duration and impact of the construction site (dust, noise, rubbish, transportation, etc.), obtained through the use of by using a system of wooden modules. The project received the product of copper mesh led to the awarding of the 2007 International Tecu Award , for use of copper in architecture.

From the point of view of energy, the design strategy pivots on the performance of the shell and on the use of an air/water heat pump, which not only produces hot water for sanitary purposes, but also feeds the heating system using radiant panels.

The system is completed by an accumulation reservoir with a capacity of 1,500 liters (about 400 gallons). M.M.

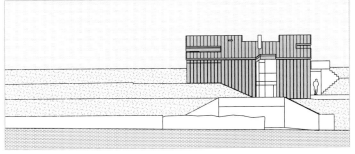

196 bottom The house is installed on the terrain forming a level that runs parallel to the the slope. A significant portion of the building is recessed into the ground, limiting the visual impact of the new construction.

196-197 The emerging part of the dwelling results in a volume marked by deep cuts, which articulate its surfaces and multiply its aspects.

197 bottom Seen from the valley, the structure appears extremely compact, marked only by the four deep openings fashioned in the façades.

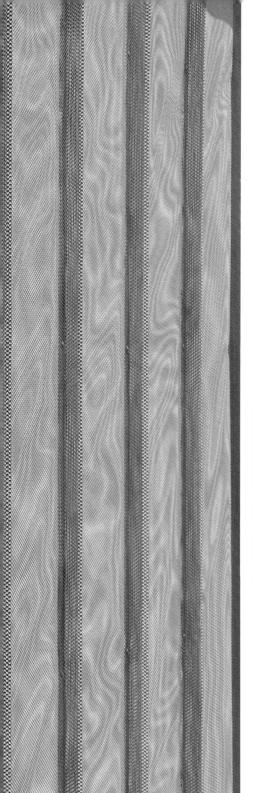

199 top On the upper floor, the day zone develops into a large open space, directly connected with the swimming pool and exterior. Bedrooms and service facilities are located in the rooms facing uphill.

199 bottom The building appears to be composed of a series of volumes separated by the previously described "cuts." The result minimizes the visual impact of the new construction.

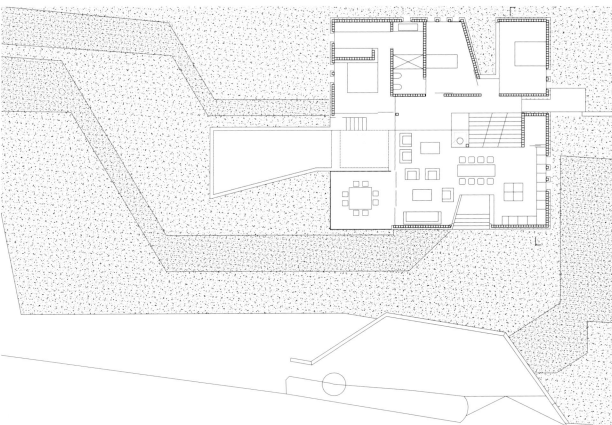

198-199 The external shell was realized using elements of copper mesh, which create a changing play of light and shadow that almost makes the surface seem to movein movement.

198 bottom The same elements in copper mesh enclose the porch, an intermediate space between interior and exterior.

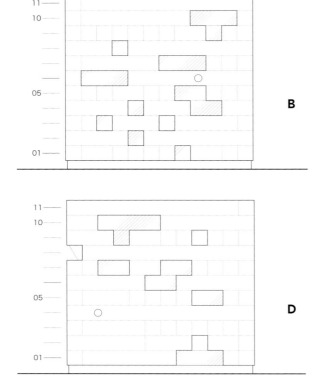

A

B

C

D

Final Wooden House

KUMAMURA, JAPAN

"I wanted to create a wooden house that would be able to have the last word on this topic." And wood – the material project planner Sou Fujimoto himself defined as "marvelously versatile" – ended up getting the upper hand over architecture itself: Final Wooden House is not a work of architecture. It is wood, material in its pure state practically.

It is not even actually a house, but rather a bungalow with minimal furnishings, realized for a forestry sciences association in a wooded region of the prefecture of Kumamoto near the village of Kumamura. In the words of Fujimoto, again, it is something extremely primitive, archetypical, and at the same time totally new, a hypothesis of architecture, but not yet a work of architecture, a process arrested at the stage in which there is only the material, with its physical characteristics, its structural and thermal performance, its surface quality, its aroma.

In this apparently haphazard piling up of large cedar trunks squared into sections of 350 mm (about 14 in) per side, there is no differentiation between structure and interior partitions, between façade elements and cover elements. We are in the presence of something very different than what we normally mean when we speak about architecture using wood: here, with the identical material, we obtain all at once structure, insulation, vertical and horizontal interior surfaces, and all the furnishings.

It is useless, even, to seek reassuring elements such as floors, attics, ceilings, walls, rooms: the only closed room is the bathroom, while the remaining space is defined in the negative; it is the volume left free, in the play of the superposition of beams, piled upon one another or bolted together. A bed area,

C

B

D

A

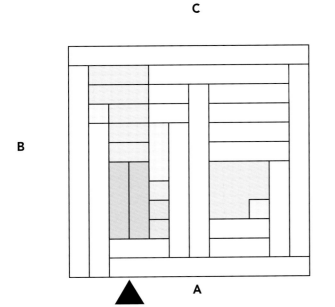

200-201 The Final Wooden House emerges from the vegetation in a protected natural environment of particular value in the prefecture of Kumamoto in the south of Japan.

200 bottom The façades of this wooden cube seem to be generated by a haphazard placement of large squared cedar trunks.

201 top The openings fashioned in the façades originate from the very arrangement of the wooden elements.

201 bottom Seen from the cover, the aspect of the building does not change: here the gray halftone screens indicate the glassed parts that provide the natural light that illuminates the interiors.

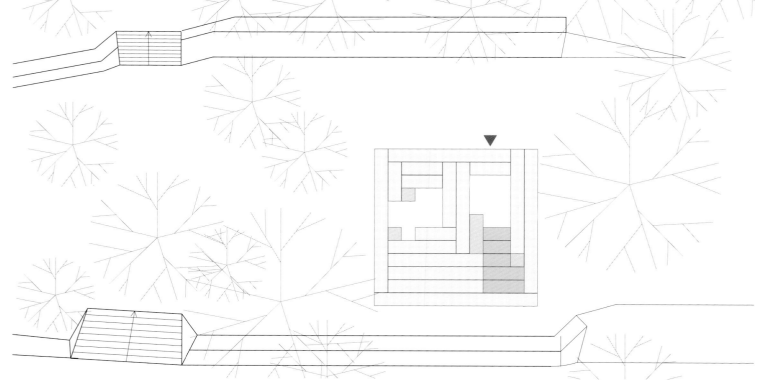

a kitchen with dining table, and a living room area have been fashioned here. But still, these are nomenclature, terms that sound improper.

The result is one of great suggestiveness, for the warmth that these surfaces transmit and for the sense of intimacy and "domestic informality," with broad spaces alternating continuously with out-of-the-way corners. The only element besides wood , there is another element in the project that plays a determining role in the structure – to the extent that it could be considered a material –"material" in this construction: is light. On the façade and on the cover, the beams are superposed in such a manner as to leave loopholes or broader open areas of irregular form, closed by simple glass panes without frames.

The experience of living in the Final Wooden House – a cube of wood and glass, about 4.4 m (about 14.4 ft) per side, fixed to a base of reinforced cement – is one of freedom of utilization, one that leaves up to the user the possibility of reinventing indefinitely the significance of each portion of space, allowing a "three-dimensional creativity" entirely out of the ordinary in our dwellings. More than an idea for a work of architecture, it is a concrete hypothesis for the use of space, beyond patterns and rules, preconfiguring almost a new way of living.

Final Wooden House is one step beyond the most innovative ideas regarding what we call a house. M.M.

---

202 top The house rises near a larger structure, to which it is subsidiary, near the bank of a creek.

202-203 The interior space offers few clues for recognizing areas dedicated to particular

functions. Even though the space is limited, it offers considerable freedom of use.

203 top The glass, mounted without framing, is the only other material that defines the exterior face of this building-prototype.

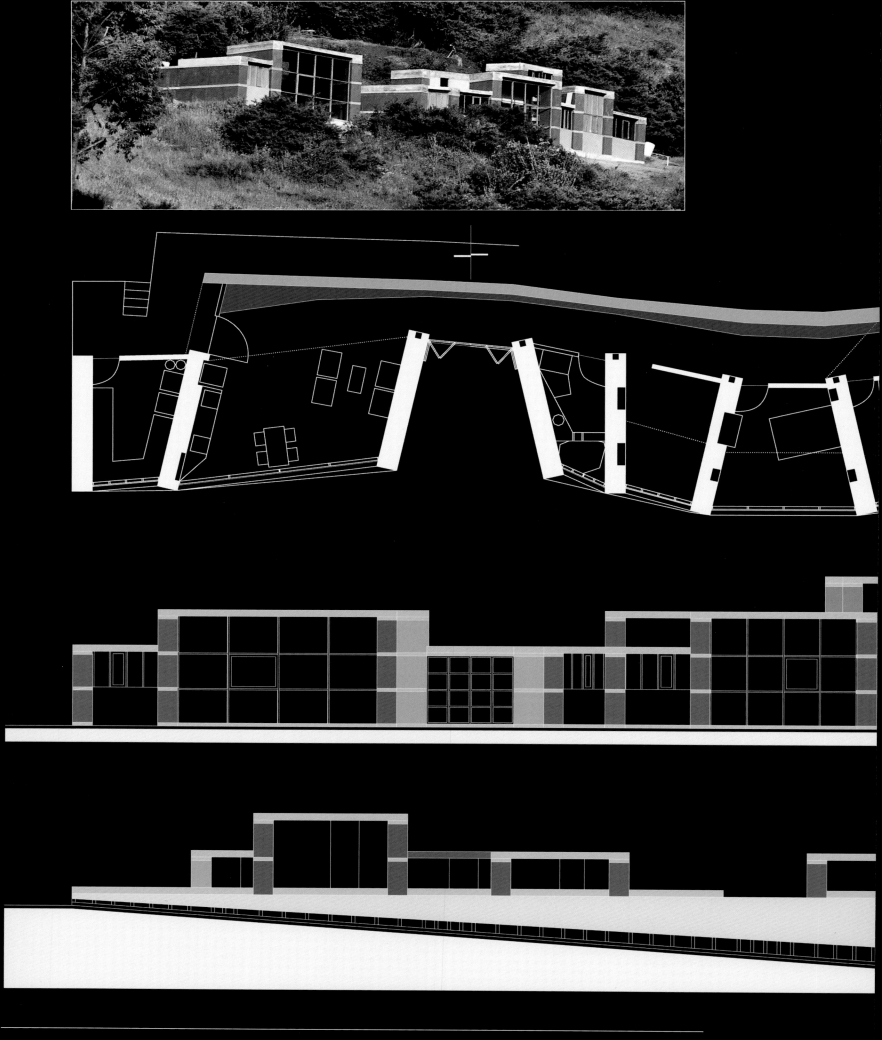

204 top The house is introduced into the slope of the Ilalò volcano, presenting itself as a jagged structure with continuous differences of height and alignment.

204-205 The irregular placement of thick walls of tamped raw earth the planimetry was conceived to reduce the risk of the house collapsing in the event of an earthquake.

Casa Entre Muros

TUMBACO, ECUADOR

In the words of its founders, young Ecuadorian architects David Barragán and Pascual Gangotena, albordE arquitectos is a collective dedicated to researching architectural-constructional strategies to optimize the recycling and recovery of materials. This theme informs a perspective of sustainability that integrates and harmonizes social, economic, and environmental aspects.

The Casa Entre Muros was realized between 2007 and 2008 at Tumbaco in the hills some 15 km (9 mi) from the capital, Quito, an area of constantly temperate climes with a landscape of luxuriant vegetation. The critical elements of the program are: living in contact with nature, close to though sheltered from the metropolitan chaos; ensuring autonomy for each of three family members; and working within a limited budget.

The terrain, on a slope of the volcano Ilalò, lies between two streams and offers spectacular views of the underlying valley.

The house faces west and curves with the land.

The building is separated from the slope by a long covered hallway that connects all the spaces in the house and also keeps most of the structure above ground, thus avoiding

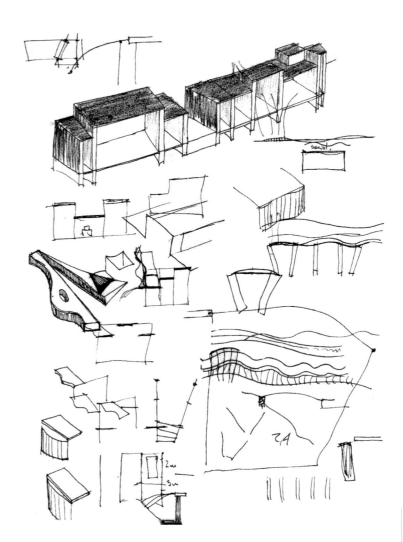

205 bottom The façade toward the valley presents grand glass-paned openings, while the façade facing the mountain is marked by the cut corresponding to the long interior corridor separating the house from the steeply sloping terrain.

ALBORDE ARQUITECTOS

problems caused by rising moisture.

The interior spaces are defined by 10 large bearing walls realized in rammed earth (pisé). The necessary material was recovered from the excavation required for creating the basement serving as foundation for the construction. The material – extracted directly from the site and therefore strictly at "zero kilometers" (in this case even "zero meters") – has extraordinary characteristics that regulate temperature and moisture for the interior spaces. The irregularly angled bearing walls, as can be seen on the plan, were conceived to limit the

"domino effect" that parallel walls would have produced in the event of signs of life – apparently not infrequent – from the volcano.

The use of natural local materials is not restricted to the soil: stone and wood are utilized in ways that extol their nature and characteristics. Left as much as possible in its natural appearance, wood is utilized in combination with pampas grass in the structure of the cover and in certain wall plugs, especially along the corridor connecting the interior and exterior spaces of the dwelling. In order to avoid use

of anti-parasite treatments, attention was given to cutting the wood at the most favorable lunar phase.

Exposed natural stone is used decoratively in the retaining wall defining the boundary against the slope toward the east.

The fragmentation of the volume reflects not only distributional requirements but also the intent to minimize the visual impact of the new construction upon the landscape. One further form of respect for the site – to honor the wishes of the commissioning party – was a traditional ceremony requesting the volcano's permission for the construction. M.M.

206 Here raw earth, stone, cement, and wood are materials for as well as for finishing as well as building. The natural appearance of these elements is never concealed, outside or in.

206-207 The interior connecting corridor is the long axis around which all the spaces are distributed, separated from one another by thick walls of tamped raw earth.

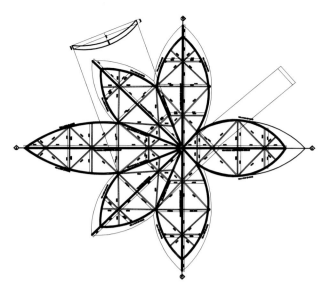

Casa Folha

ANGRA DOS REIS, BRAZIL

Ivo Mareines and Rafael Patalano took inspiration from the natural forms of the leaf and the spiral for this luxurious residence, with the intent of integrating the house closely with the surrounding environment. The image of the tropical house facing the sea recalls the strong interaction between man and nature, which resolves into a spatial and visual fluidity between the interior and the external environment. And in this case, it translates into a continuous succession of spaces without need for intermediary zones, aspiring to absolute transparency toward the exterior. This planimetric arrangement, completed toward the exterior by grand verandas separated from the interiors by broad sliding glass windows, makes the building ideal for parties and receptions, as requested by the commissioners. The carefully placed greenery contributes to the intense dialogue between garden and dwelling, as can be seen in the case of the swimming pool that insinuates itself beneath the construction, crosses the dining room, and then becomes a habitat for fish and aquatic plants, with the veranda planned for the back of the building facing onto it.

The unmistakable signature of this architectural work is its covering, with an organic design: a series of leaves that gives the project its name. This symbolizes the search for connection between the interior and exterior spaces of the dwelling, taking as cultural reference the Brazilian vernacular architecture. This style has always employed the roof as an element in handling the hot-humid climate typical of the tropical zone by means of bioclimatic solutions using passive

208-209 The name of the building takes its origin from the form of the roof, a leaf composed of six lobes to shade the six sections of the home.

209 top The sketch depicting the structural elements of the roof recalls illustrations used in botany to show the biological growth of leaves.

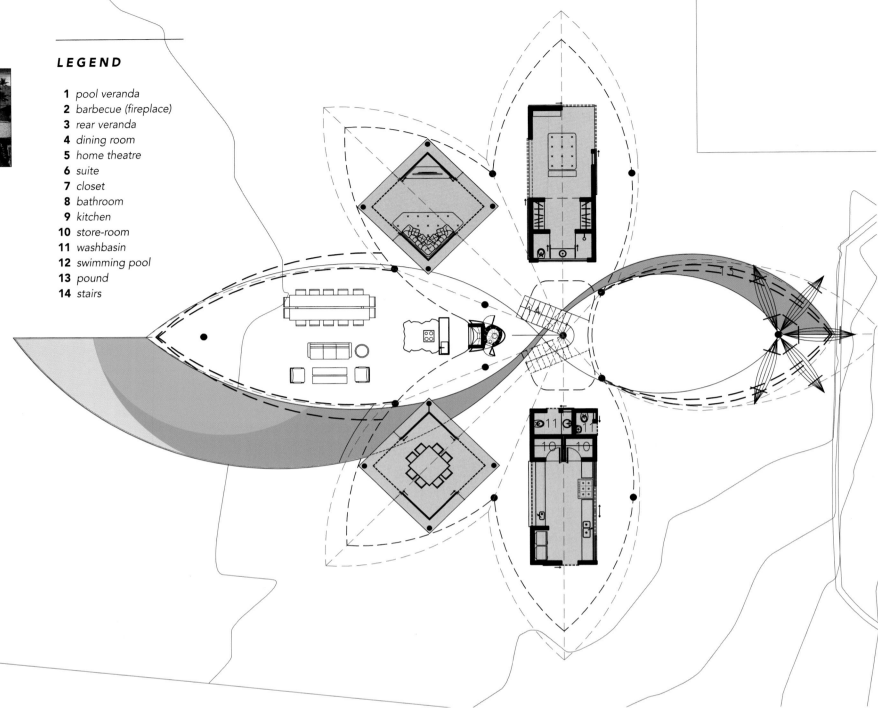

LEGEND

1 pool veranda
2 barbecue (fireplace)
3 rear veranda
4 dining room
5 home theatre
6 suite
7 closet
8 bathroom
9 kitchen
10 store-room
11 washbasin
12 swimming pool
13 pound
14 stairs

cooling techniques. Just like a large leaf, the expansive covering serves to protect the interior from the sun's heat and light, whereas the ample heights (from 3 to 9 m; from 9.8 ft to 29.5 ft) and the exterior walls, which can be opened almost completely, allow fresh air coming from the sea to circulate into the interior, passively cooling the dwelling spaces. The rainwater falling onto the large covering is gathered into a central channel so it can be reused to flush toilets and water the garden.

The roof used lamellate elements of eucalyptus wood from managed forests, allowing very broad lighting and, at the same time, presenting a pleasant aesthetic appearance. The covering is lined with shingles of *Pinus Taeda* to handle the distinctly curvilinear profile of the six "leaves" composing it. Reference to nature continues in the choice of materials for coverings, which, with the exception of the glass and the COR-TEN steel, are all local in origin: slate slabs, bamboo, indigenous species of wood from controlled forests, earthy flooring, and wooden posts recovered from outdated electrical lines. B.S.

210 top The ground floor plan shows how the large roof, at this level, reunites different functions, enclosed by transparent walls which can be opened, for the most part, or placed into the open in the shade of the two porches crossed by a reflecting pool.

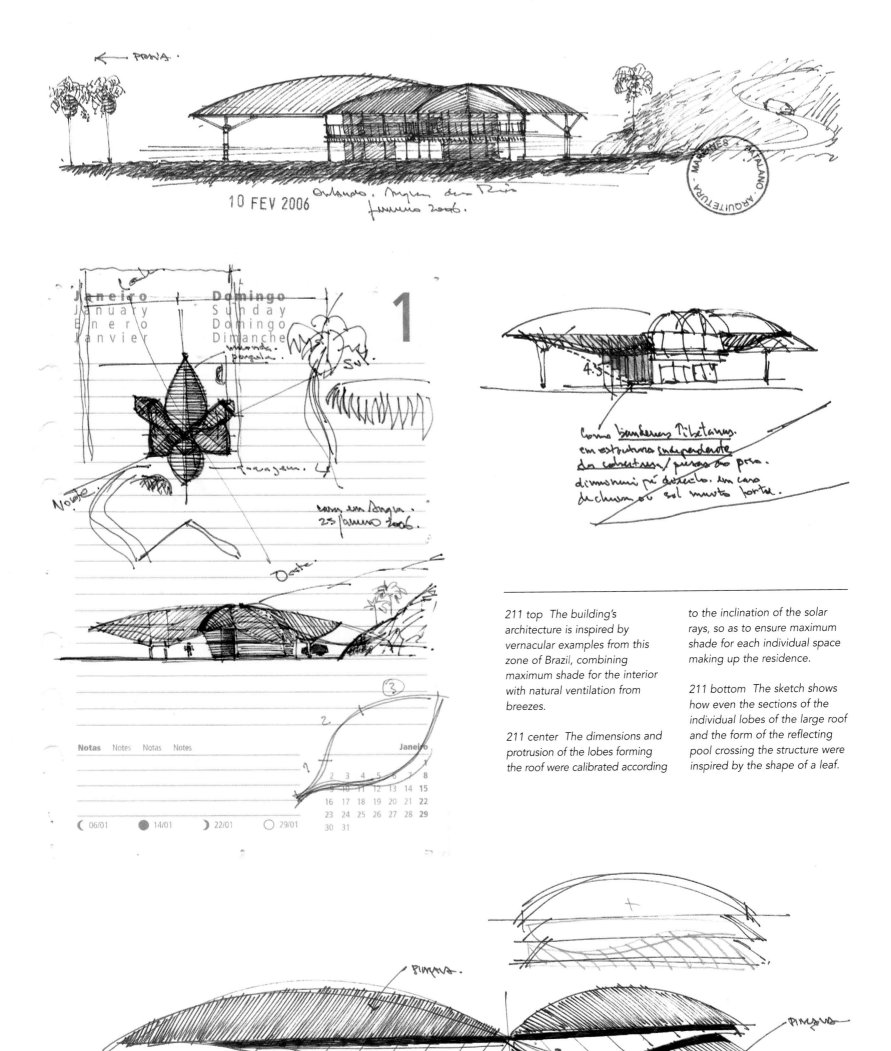

211 top The building's architecture is inspired by vernacular examples from this zone of Brazil, combining maximum shade for the interior with natural ventilation from breezes.

211 center The dimensions and protrusion of the lobes forming the roof were calibrated according to the inclination of the solar rays, so as to ensure maximum shade for each individual space making up the residence.

211 bottom The sketch shows how even the sections of the individual lobes of the large roof and the form of the reflecting pool crossing the structure were inspired by the shape of a leaf.

212 bottom The plan of the first
level and the two sections shows
how the lobes of the roof not
covering the double height
porches contain the four
bedrooms reserved for guests,
each outfitted with its own
bathroom.

212-213 The rooms of the upper
floors face one another via a
balcony opening onto the private
porch, where a few hammocks
rock, suspended over the
reflecting pool that connects it
with the garden.

213 bottom The building is
surrounded by a vast, luxuriant
garden, which receives the
majority of its water from the rain
gathered on the large roof.

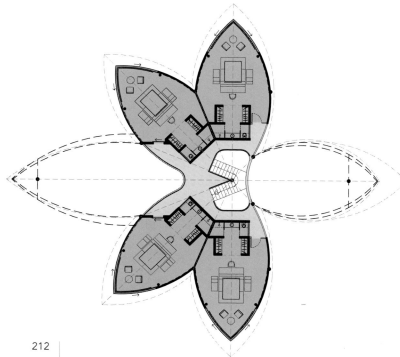

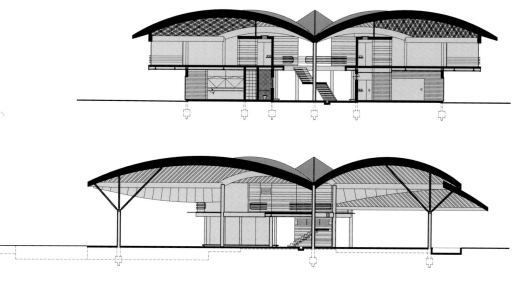

214 The "public" porch functions as an open living room, facing onto a reflecting pool, which renders its microclimate more agreeable.

214-215 A nighttime view of the building highlights the extreme transparency of the rooms facing the garden and central porch.

216 top *The ground floor sitting room is enclosed by transparent walls and protected from the sun, typically intense in this part of the world, by means of the floor profile of the upper level, which repeats the shape of the roof.*

216 bottom One of the upper floor bedrooms, showing how the wooden structure of the roof remains apparent. The transparent walls are screened by heavy draperies of colored fabric.

216-217 The large "public" porch, designed for the owners' parties, is the heart of the house and constitutes the principal view for the majority of the dwelling's rooms.

1M Village House

TINOS, GREECE

Born in 2004, mXarchitecture is a Paris studio directed by Emmanuel Choupis. In his still brief portfolio of works brought to completion, this vacation home realized at Tinos stands out. Completed in 2009, it was designed to house a family of three, and occasionally friends and relatives. The functional program, whose hallmark is flexibility, induced the planners to configure a complex residential organism – an aggregate of cells – that recalls a small traditional village more than it does a single dwelling.

The extremely severe regulations for safeguarding the landscape on this small island among the Cyclades were seen by the planners as an important stimulus rather than a limitation. As in a village, private spaces alternate with communal ones, arranged over multiple levels and following the form of the terrain. Upon the lot, still showing vestiges of pre-existing constructions – stone walls, a wine press, a stone oven – three graduated platforms are structured, sloping downward to follow the incline of the terrain. The weave of the pre-existing fabric is resumed and enhanced by the succession of voids and fills that develops along up-and-down itineraries, which, in turn, form the roadway network connecting the spaces. The structures themselves, of varying heights and dimensions, are used to reinforce this image, with the highest tower marking the edge of the house-village.

From the functional and distributional point of view, emphasis was placed on ensuring maximum autonomy for the three bedrooms with bathrooms, with each dwelling unit characterized by a different shape and independent of the collective spaces – open kitchen, living room and dining room – housed in the central volume.

Constructional technologies and materials make reference, to the greatest extent possible, to the resources available on=site. To work the local stone used in building the thick

218 top The irregular plan is marked by the massive stone walls, remnants, in part, from pre-existing constructions that have been judiciously integrated into the new building.

218-219 At Tinos, the norms for safeguarding the landscape are particularly severe, but this has only made the task all the more

stimulating for the project planner, who succeeded in making best use of the capabilities of the local artisans.

219 bottom A building that seems to have been part of the place forever; the dry mounted stone walls are as much a characteristic of Tinos's rural landscape as the traditional structures.

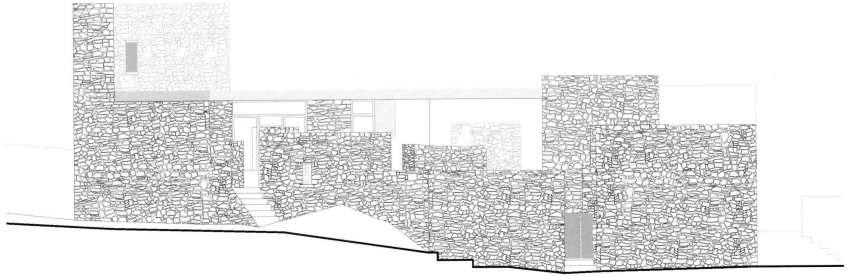

bearing walls, highly qualified craftsmen – repositories of refined technical knowledge steeped in tradition – were employed. The flat coverings are realized in exposed, reinforced cement, with an unhewn aspect that harmonizes well with the roughness of the stone surfaces. All the floorings, also, are in cement, a single-material usage that underscores the fluidity and continuity between external and internal spaces. The arrangement of the structural elements automatically defines the location and form of the openings, which can be glass-paneled or plugged by elements of natural wood or marble.

The use of stone and reinforced cement is a determining element in the bio-climatic strategies applied in the building: the thermal inertia of these massive elements minimizes the impact of external temperature changes. In a Mediterranean climate, the capacity of materials to slow the heating process provides natural interior cooling system, making heating equipment unnecessary. The effect is further enhanced by the arrangement of the openings, which provide cross-ventilation throughout.

Reducing the separation between the various locales exalts the spatial continuity between inside and outside, maximizing livability for all the spaces of this house-village. The basin at the center of the composition, besides functioning as swimming pool and component of the micro-climatic-control system, further emphasizes the character of this operation, which proposes anew the principle of growth around water that typifies the settlement patterns of Tinos's inhabited centers. M.M.

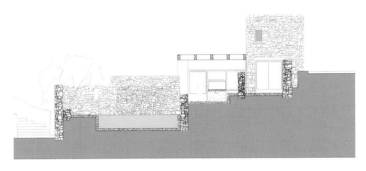

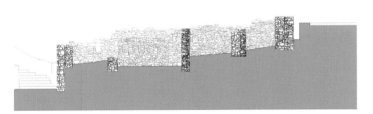

220 top Closed, open, and partially open spaces succeed one another with fluidity, just as the fusion is total among parts of pre-existing constructions and parts of the new realization.

220 center To erect the new building, remnants of the existing walls were reutilized, as highlighted by the two sections representing the starting and ending situations.

220 bottom The process of construction appears even clearer in the diagrams bottom: the building organism grows upon the "root" of what existed previously.

221 On this Mediterranean island, settlements historically have developed around the water, and so does this new building; the curved wall on the first floor is an old bread oven.

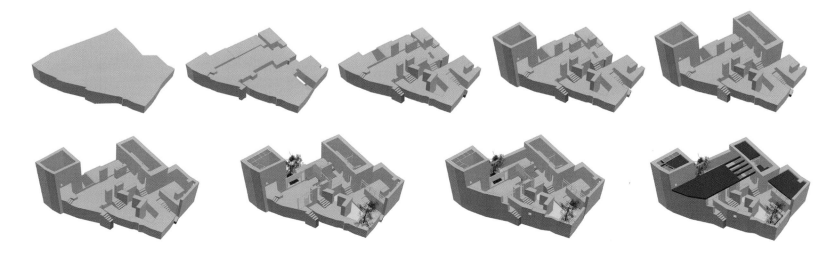

222 The master bedroom is situated in the "tower" marking the north corner of the complex. A great cut in the roof floods this space with natural light.

222-223 Tinos's climate suggests solutions like the one adopted for the dining room: a large outside table whose surface continues inside, becoming a work surface for the kitchen.

223 top left e right The living room, kitchen and dining room constitute a single large space, which develops partly inside and partly outside the building. Visible cement, plastered walls and dry-mounted stone walls characterized the interiors.

matteo thun *(vigilius mountain reso* *(hamadryade lodge)* - ryntovt design *(wisa wooden design hotel)* - 24h archite

living ecologically is also...

t) - donnet tresse architectes
iendhouse hotel) - pieta-linda auttila
ture *(ecological children's activity center).*

living ecologically is also...

Tourism is one of the primary sectors in the world's economy, and in the last 30 years it has been a frenzied consumer of energy and resources. Owing to its expansion, it has attracted continual investments, fueling an industry whose principal destinations include the marvels of nature, and whose activities exercise a strong environmental impact. Tourism demands architecture for temporary lodging, which can have major implications from the ecological point of view since the industry is driven by financial entities whose primary purpose is to maximize profits in a short period of time. For this reason, the World Tourism Organization (WTO) in 1988 coined the principle of "sustainable tourism," according to which "tourist activities are sustainable when they develop in such a way as to be able to maintain the vitality of a tourist area for an unlimited time, they do not alter the environment (natural, social, artistic), and they do not impede or inhibit development of other social and economic activities." In 1995 at a world conference in Lanzarote, Canary Islands, Spain, the WTO, together with UNESCO and the European Commission, signed the Charter for Sustainable Tourism, proclaiming three fundamental objectives: protection of the natural environment in which life takes place, solid economic development, and greater social equity. Sustainability should not translate into renouncement or limitation for the tourist, but rather should represent an added value allowing the experience of appreciation and full respect for the beauty of the places, involving all the senses, including that of responsibility. The decision to build a "sustainable" tourist structure can also become a marketing tool to attract travelers who wish to embrace other cultures.

Reconciling nature with culture should be the principal theme inspiring project planning and management of structures for hospitality. The concept of sustainability possesses a twofold merit: on the one side is a merely ecological question, which involves conserving the balance of all components of the natural environment (flora, fauna, sources of water, etc.); on the other is the anthropological question, which can be interpreted as maintenance of and respect for the local culture and economy. In developed countries, this means cooperation with local companies, short distances for provisioning, and integration with the chain of local added value. In underdeveloped areas, the problem is much more complex and it is necessary to do much more. Defense of the environment in this case means respect for farming terrains, the water cycle, nutritional habits, local public and private architecture, and use of free time. In these contexts, creating new structures for travelers can facilitate the dialogue between local inhabitants, protective of their culture, and visitors who want to learn about it. A case in point is the Hamadryade Lodge, created in the middle of the virgin forest of Ecuador by two French entrepreneurs with the objective of respecting the culture of their hosts, the aborigines, by safeguarding and diffusing their store of knowledge about medicinal uses of plants. From their lodge built with local materials, the entrepreneurs organize guided visits into the forest to make their customers feel at home in nature. They also donate a portion of their earnings to projects promoted by local communities.

From the strictly architectural point of view, one way to reduce environmental impact is to build small structures that can harmonize with the natural landscape and/or constructed areas. Inspiration should come, if possible, from local constructional tradition (without mimicking it), limiting consumption of ground space whenever possible, and utilizing materials that reduce environmental impact. Structures for hospitality are measured in terms of the landscape of the place – natural as well as constructed – making use of local materials so as to integrate the structures as much as possible into their surroundings and build with nature. The majority of the examples showcased in this section of the book are immersed in uncontaminated natural contexts; the dialogue with their environment is pursued by using local building materials and techniques.

At the luxurious Soneva Kiri resort on the remote island of Koh Kood in eastern Thailand, the center hosting activities for children is a structure with an organic form. It obeys the rules of local architecture, maintaining a desirable interior climate using natural means, and using native techniques for construction in bamboo; the Dutch project planners consulted a team of local artisans for the latter. Analogously, FriendHouse Hotel, a small eco hotel in the woods of Ukraine, has organic forms echoing the vernacular and constructional traditions of the place. In both cases, integrating the construction into the contrasting landscape was a formidable task, obvious even in the sense of welcoming afforded by the use of natural materials – a must for making guests feel at home. Even the Wisa wooden hotel, a temporary vacation lodging module erected in Helsinki, Finland, depended upon the use of locally derived wood. Using this exclusively, architect Pieta-Linda Auttila produced a building capable of harmonizing with either urban or natural surroundings. Guests would need to be adaptable since the building, more like an embellished campsite than a hotel, provides no electricity or running water.

This latter project could even be interpreted as a provocative response to the huge environmental impact of hospitality structures because of the unsustainable quantities of energy, water, and products consumed inside them to provide maximum comfort for customers. Hotels must be made to operate using principles of energy efficiency, exploiting the precious contribution from renewable sources, and reducing as much as possible their own emissions into the environment. Exemplary in this sense is the Hotel Vigilius, designed by Matteo Thun and constructed on the San Vigilio peak near Merano in Italy's South Tyrol. Accessible only on foot or by cable car, all of its features – even its distinctive profile – were designed for maximum energy efficiency. Boasting an efficient insulating system, a controlled heat-recovery ventilation system, and a biomass heating installation, it taps the spring water from Monte San Vigilio itself. B.S.

Vigilius Mountain Resort

MONTE SAN VIGILIO, ITALY

A luxury resort completely immersed in mountain beauty, designed expressly for contemplation of the Alpine landscape at 1500 m (4921 ft) altitude, demonstrating total harmony between nature and constructions. Matteo Thun achieved this result by taking inspiration from nature herself. This is why the new building recalls a gigantic tree trunk reclining on the ground, and recalls, as well, the character and materials of traditional local architecture, albeit translated into contemporary forms. The architect's charge called for expanding a pre-existing receptive structure, contained in a building dating from the early 1900s, in perfect *Kärntener* style and conserving its original features. Like the resort, it can be reached only by foot or the nearby cableway.

The design for the new hotel assumed as primary theme the concept of balance, sought in the relationship between architecture and nature, as in the dialogue between the interior spaces and the exterior panorama, and the relationship between the existing structure and the newly constructed building. The latter was built of wood, using a highly insulated, prefabricated structure that develops in length along the north-south axis, with two floors above ground and one below, realized, in turn, in reinforced cement concrete. The new building communes with the outdoors by means of a series of wooden terraces situated to correspond with the most important common spaces (restaurant, lounge, conference pavilion, swimming pool), thus allowing appreciation of different views of the landscape. The 25 rooms and six suites face east or west, and are distributed over the ground floor and upper floor. The rooms are finished and furnished in minimalist style, recalling the simplicity of nature and using natural materials such as wood, raw clay, and the sunlight entering through broad, glass-paneled walls. These latter are equipped, all along the length of the building, with wooden fillets that can be regulated, thus permitting a noteworthy passive input, reducing the demand for heating by exploiting solar energy. This system strongly marks the appearance of the outer faces of the building, and at the same time allows the windows to be shaded during the hot season, limiting energy consumption for cooling,

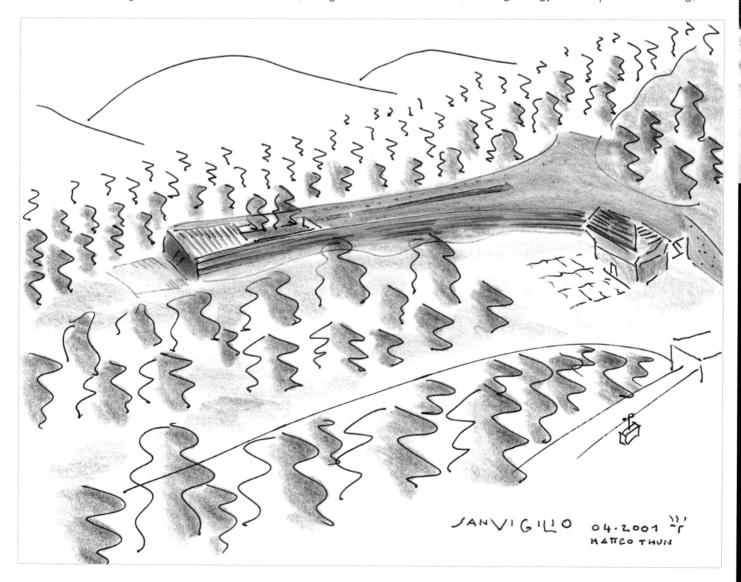

SANVIGILIO 04.2001
MATTEO THUN

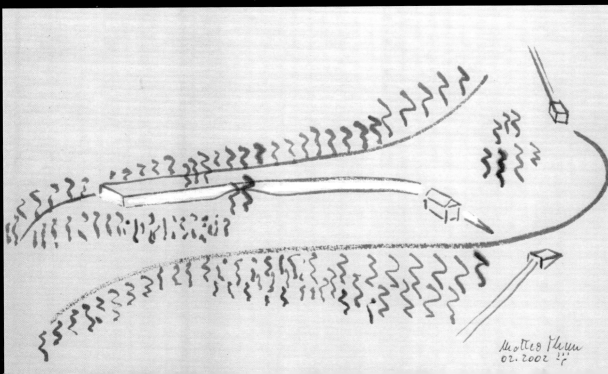

228 and 229 bottom The project presents itself as the integration of a small pre-existing structure with a new building that, in spite of its significant size, respects the natural surroundings by enriching the panorama.

228-229 The new structure's long, transparent walls are complemented by a screening of horizontal wooden fillets, inspired by tree bark and adequately protecting the interior from the sun.

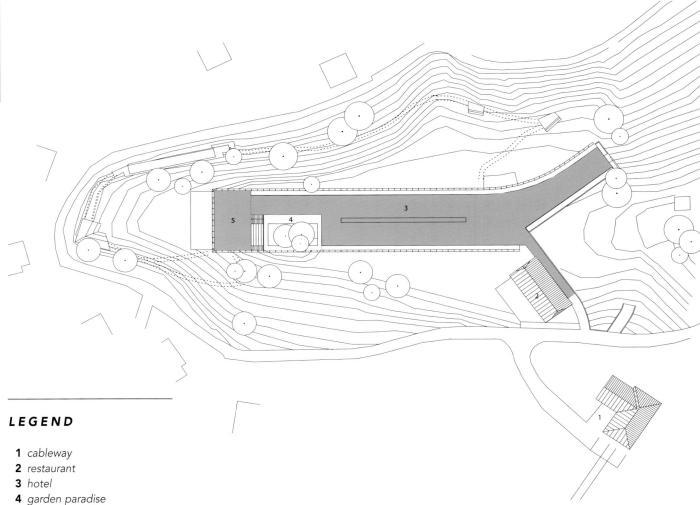

LEGEND

1 cableway
2 restaurant
3 hotel
4 garden paradise
5 swimming pool

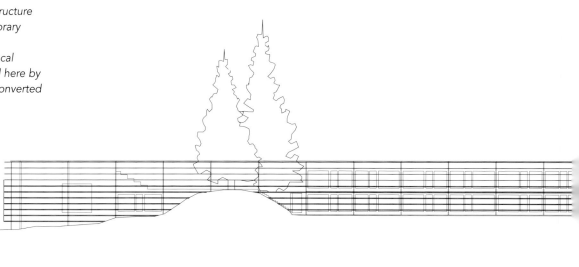

which is further reduced by the green covering that prevents overheating of this part of the exterior shell. Special attention was given to the interior climate. It was decided to air-condition the building using radiant installations contained in special raw clay walls in the rooms; these serve also to accumulate passive heat from the windows and to enhance the aesthetic character of the space. The hotel is also equipped with a controlled heat-recovery ventilation system, which maintains the interior air quality and, at the same time, reduces the amount of energy needed for heating, produced by a biomass furnace.

The multiple energy-saving devices, matched with significantly insulated opaque structures and double-paned glass, have reduced the primary energy requirement for heating the building to 30 kWh per sq m (2.8 kWh per sq ft) per year.   B.S.

230 top The new volume adapts to the conformation of the natural plateau and to the positions of the pre-existing buildings, represented by the refuge and the cableway station.

230-231 top The new structure reinterprets, in contemporary style, the characters and materials of traditional local architecture, represented here by the pre-existing refuge converted into a bar-restaurant.

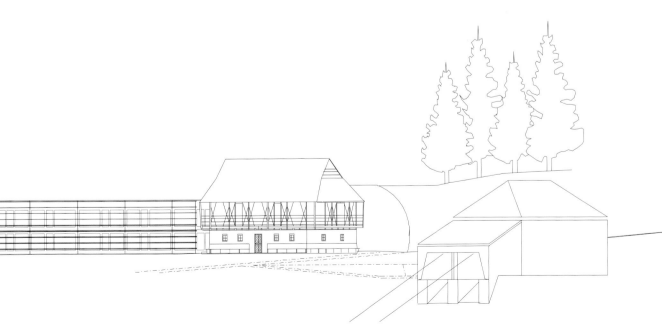

230-231 bottom The prospect of the resort is highly elongated, as suggested by the form of the lot and also by the desire to give each room an ample transparent aspect.

day

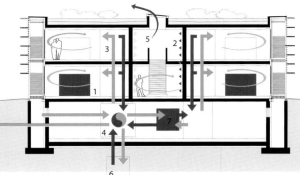

clima section
(mechanical ventilation, natural/earth
heating and cooling/heated walls

heat recovery 85%

night

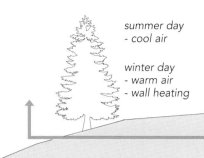

summer day
- cool air

winter day
- warm air
- wall heating

summer night
- light warm air

winter night
- warm air
- wall heating

LEGEND

1 wall of raw earth with radiant installation
2 wall-mounted radiant heating system

3 air distribution
4 heat-recovery controlled ventilation system
5 hot air output

6 underground heat accumulation system
7 low-temperature heating system

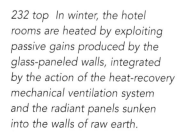

232 top In winter, the hotel rooms are heated by exploiting passive gains produced by the glass-paneled walls, integrated by the action of the heat-recovery mechanical ventilation system and the radiant panels sunken into the walls of raw earth.

232-233 At one end of the new building is a large glass-paneled wall enclosing the well-being center and the covered swimming pool, offering a clear view of the surrounding woods.

233 top In summer, the wooden brise-soleil blocks incoming sunlight while the raw earth walls absorb excessive heat during the day and restore it at night.

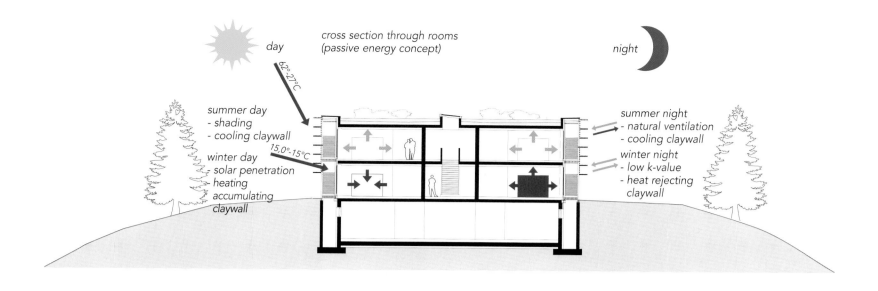

day

cross section through rooms
(passive energy concept)

night

62°-27°C

summer day
- shading
- cooling claywall

15,0°-15°C

winter day
- solar penetration
- heating
  accumulating
  claywall

summer night
- natural ventilation
- cooling claywall

winter night
- low k-value
- heat rejecting
  claywall

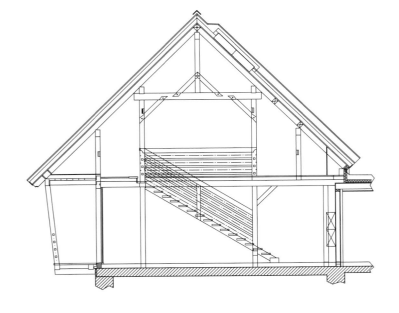

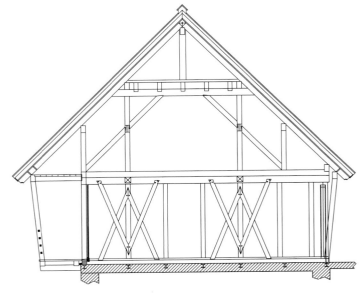

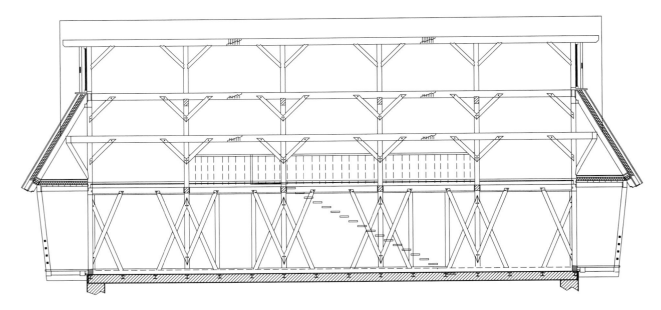

234 top The original building, dating from the early 20th century, was restored by maintaining the original features of the Corinthian style wooden architecture.

234 center The resort's restaurant occupies the upper floors of the pre-existing refuge, one of which has a broad glass-paneled wall allowing a view of the surrounding panorama even on the coldest days.

234 bottom The section shows how the functions contained in the pre-existing building are connected to the new portion of the resort by means of a two-story corridor, glass-paneled for the most part.

235 The refuge was modernized by introducing a transparent section to highlight the most widespread forms of the wooden building system used in local vernacular architecture.

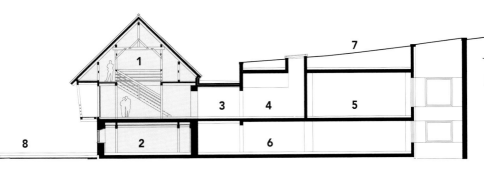

LEGEND
1 restaurant
2 stube
3 entryway
4 reception
5 office
6 warehouse/service locales
7 green roof
8 terrace

236-237 The natural beauty surrounding the resort is reflected in the mirror of the panoramic swimming pool of spring water thanks to the broad glass-paneled walls.

236 bottom The corridors for accessing the rooms receive natural light through a series of nithal skylights. The natural light is diffused throughout the rooms by means of the soft, warm colors on the walls, creating a welcoming atmosphere.

237 bottom The resort's common living room is particularly welcoming on account of its fireplace and the palette of natural materials with which it is covered and furnished.

238-239 One of the four bungalows making up the structure is immersed, like the other three, in a luxuriant garden ensuring maximum privacy for the guests.

238 bottom The walls of each bungalow can, for the most part, be opened to allow guests the possibility of enjoying nature and, at the same time, ensuring maximum ventilation for the interior and improving its microclimate.

Hamadryade Lodge

VENECIA-MISAHUALLI, ECUADOR

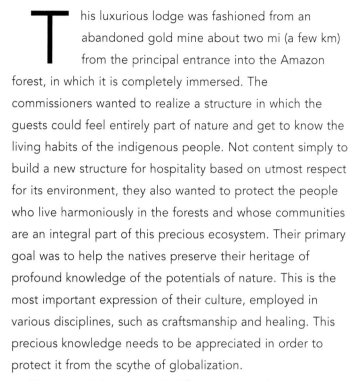

This luxurious lodge was fashioned from an abandoned gold mine about two mi (a few km) from the principal entrance into the Amazon forest, in which it is completely immersed. The commissioners wanted to realize a structure in which the guests could feel entirely part of nature and get to know the living habits of the indigenous people. Not content simply to build a new structure for hospitality based on utmost respect for its environment, they also wanted to protect the people who live harmoniously in the forests and whose communities are an integral part of this precious ecosystem. Their primary goal was to help the natives preserve their heritage of profound knowledge of the potentials of nature. This is the most important expression of their culture, employed in various disciplines, such as craftsmanship and healing. This precious knowledge needs to be appreciated in order to protect it from the scythe of globalization.

The commissioners needed first to reorganize an area that had been destroyed for economic motives, then to create a new environment in which nature could resume her role as protagonist, displaying all the marvels she can offer. Initially the land involved in the operation was bleak, colonized only by infesting plants; these were removed to make space for endemic species that could regenerate the land. Today the lodge, composed of four bungalows isolated from each other and equipped with service facilities and balconies, is immersed in a luxuriant garden populated by birds, butterflies, and small animals. The complex was designed in accordance with contemporary Minimalist architectural canons. Its clean lines contrast with the profile of luxuriant nature and do not, in any manner, attempt to mimic the features of indigenous structures. These were instead used as inspiration or to devise bioclimatic solutions: allowing abundant ventilation of the buildings, regulation of the humidity of the spaces, and illumination of the interiors using natural light.

The interiors were decorated using local materials and elements from the indigenous culture, which integrate harmoniously with the clean lines of the contemporary architecture. References to nature and native cultures give each bungalow its own identity. Each ceiling displays vegetal symbols of the four most important populations. The color scheme is inspired by the Amazon forest: red earth, jewel-toned butterfly wings, green leaves and a rainbow of wildflowers.

The lodge is managed so as to create the least possible impact on surrounding nature. Water comes not from the river or the water tables, but is collected from the rains that fall abundantly here, and from the gray and black waters that are recycled by means of natural filtration.   B.S.

239 Each unit is equipped with its own private bathroom and decorated with a different motif, inspired from nature and by the culture of the indigenous people.

FriendHouse Hotel

DNEPROPETROVSK, UKRAINE

The FriendHouse Hotel is a gathering place completely immersed in the woods at the banks of the River Orel in southeast Ukraine. The project takes inspiration from natural values, making intrinsic harmony with the surrounding environment its goal. The design of the hotel is resolved, in accordance with the project planners' intentions, as an organic development, with forms suggested by the relationship the building was called upon to establish with the natural landscape in which it is immersed. This produced a perfect integration among the parts. Its symbiotic relationship with nature, combined with a pleasing array of services, renders the hotel an ideal environment in which to renew body and mind.

The most suitable place for building was chosen based on a careful analysis of the energies proper to the site, in relation to the orography of the terrain, and using techniques deriving from geobiology, whereas the materials adopted were borrowed from local constructional tradition.

The project wisely blends the linearity of Minimalist design with the soft and welcoming forms of organic architecture. These latter were employed to realize the bedrooms, integrated by linear construction on a single floor, in which the various spaces – service locales, sitting rooms, a restaurant, some open spaces for lounging, some gardens, and a parking lot – alternate, often crisscrossing with one another.

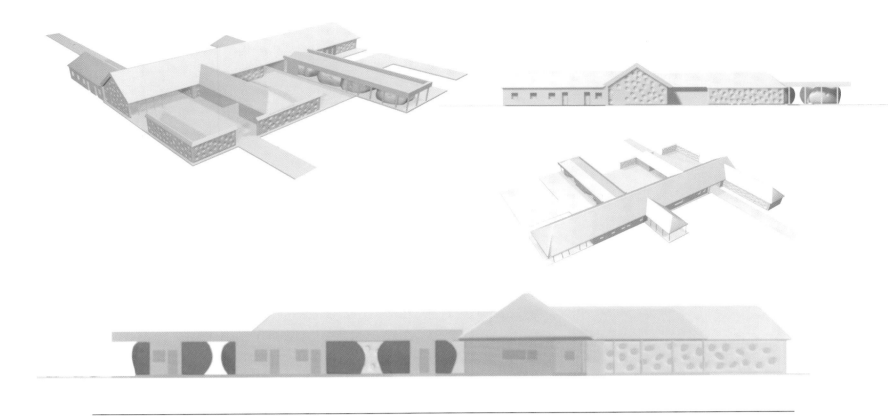

240-241 Some of the bedrooms are located in a series of curvilinear shells constructed using local vernacular architectural techniques, favoring natural materials such as wood, straw, and clay.

241 top The building is a result of the interpenetration of a series of open and closed spaces, hosting the usual functions of hotels.

The entirety occupies a total of 1750 sq m (about 18,840 sq ft), in which a significant covering of canes intersects with a simple flat roof of wood. Nearby is a garden of apple trees, planted to satisfy a local belief that a good farmer ought to receive guests at least twice a year, once in spring when the apple trees blossom, and once in summer to gather their fruit.

The materials employed in the project are all natural in origin: wood, raw earth, canes, and marble cobblestones; these latter define the exterior pavements, while the interior floors are generally covered with wood. The distinctive organic shells characterized by round openings containing the bedrooms were inspired by the vernacular constructional techniques; that is, by means of wooden structures filled with a blend of straw and clay and finished with a composition of clay and sawdust. These distinctive "bubbles" are connected to one another by a flat cover that takes the form, toward the exterior, of a wooden baseboard. The service block has a roof made of cane layers 40 cm (15.7 in) thick, ensuring optimal protection from the rain and winter cold. The wooden structure supporting this cover was intentionally left visible in the restaurant hall, so as to amplify its vertical dimension and impart a sense of liberty.   B.S.

242 The interiors of some of the rooms confirm the organic imprint of the project, visible in the particular design of the shapes as well as in the exclusive use of natural materials and furnishings.

242-243 The roof of the central structure of the restaurant is realized in wood and cane left in their natural state, in accordance with local architectural rules, making the salon seem larger.

244 The bathrooms serving the bedrooms, furnished only with elements in wood and raw clay, confirm the project planners' intention of realizing a building in complete harmony with nature.

244-245 The rooms are illuminated with both natural and artificial light through a series of irregular holes fashioned in the walls, which are constructed of wood and straw and coated with clay.

Wisa Wooden Design Hotel

HELSINKI, FINLAND

This structure, the prototype for a vacation cottage, ended up winning a competition for architecture in wood promoted by a Finnish company operating in the sector. The contest announcement allowed just 24 hours to define the project solution and five weeks to realize it. The module in question would offer lodging for the night, but no services, electricity or running water. The structure comprises two counterpoised volumes, the space dedicated to rest and the sitting room, equipped with two completely transparent, glass-paneled sides, one facing toward the sea to the east, the other toward the panorama of the city of Helsinki to the west. (The structure was set up at Valkosaari, one of the islands surrounding the city.) In both cases, the second glass-paneled wall faces a sort of inner courtyard, defined by the continuity of the shell connecting the two closed volumes. This shell expands its pattern of wooden fillets to form a side wing of organic profile, ensuring a view of the landscape and inviting natural light while still providing shelter from the wind. Natural light is a fundamental element in Finnish architecture, characterized here by inclined rays that vary continuously, orchestrating plays of light and shadow that change throughout the course of the year.

The image that inspired the project planner was that of a piece of hard candy with a soft center, one that, with each bite, reveals more of its true inner form. Others have compared the structure to a block of wood hurled against the rocks by a sea wave, causing it to split at the center and reveal its innermost secrets.

246 bottom The planimetry shows how the building is composed of two closed cells connected to one another by an interior courtyard protected by a wooden structure.

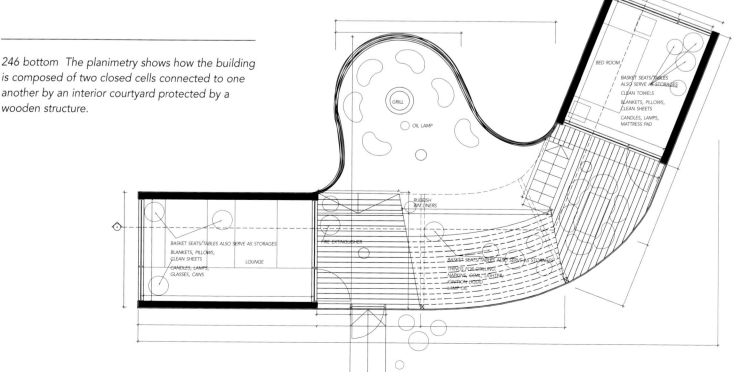

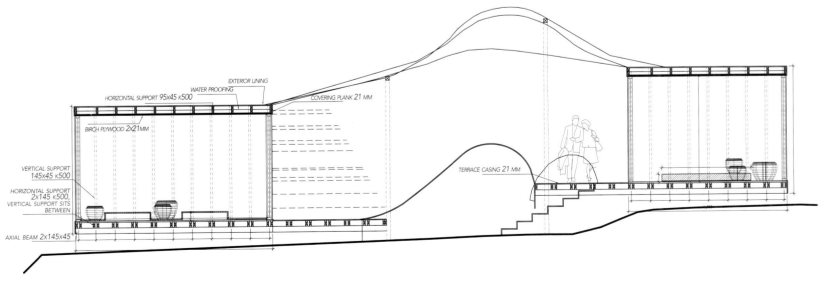

HORIZONTAL SUPPORT 95x45 K500
WATER PROOFING
EXTERIOR LINING
COVERING PLANK 21 MM

BIRCH PLYWOOD 2X21MM

VERTICAL SUPPORT
145x45 K500

HORIZONTAL SUPPORT
2x145 K500,
VERTICAL SUPPORT SITS
BETWEEN

TERRACE CASING 21 MM

AXIAL BEAM 2x145x45

246-247 The two rooms making up the dwelling module communicate through an exterior space characterized by a membrane of wooden fillets, the varying distances between them allowing exterior views at certain points.

247 bottom The various components of the structure are distributed over diverse levels so as to adapt to the different configurations of the terrain.

The structure is built entirely of wood; the gray patina of the external shell gives way to warmer tones toward the interior. The purpose of the project was to demonstrate the extreme versatility of wood as a material for architecture, functioning here not only as bearing structure but also as interior and exterior coating for the shell. The structure is of red fir, realized using standardized elements available on the market. The organic weave defining the courtyard is composed of laminated, 8 mm (0.3 in) pine boards, curved according to constructional requirements. The entire building was conceived so as to fit the construction time limit, allow the structure to be easily dismantled later, and make it possible to reassemble it at another site. The walls and ceilings are coated with birch plywood panels, while the floors are covered with planks of pine without knots. The exterior coating is treated with water-based finishes and the interiors are finished with wax. Natural light enters from both sides of the rooms, enhancing the warm colors of the materials. B.S.

248 bottom Each room has two blind walls and two glass-paneled walls, which face toward the exterior and onto the inner courtyard connecting them, thus allowing sufficient natural light.

248-249 In view of the particular conformation of the central courtyard, the two transparent ends

of the building can be oriented in various directions, depending on which exterior panorama is to be appreciated.

249 bottom The dwelling module is completely blind on the side containing the entryway, ensuring maximum privacy for guests.

250 top and bottom *The particular form of the dwelling module was inspired by a piece of candy with a soft center. At the same time, it recalls a piece of wood that has been split to reveal its core.*

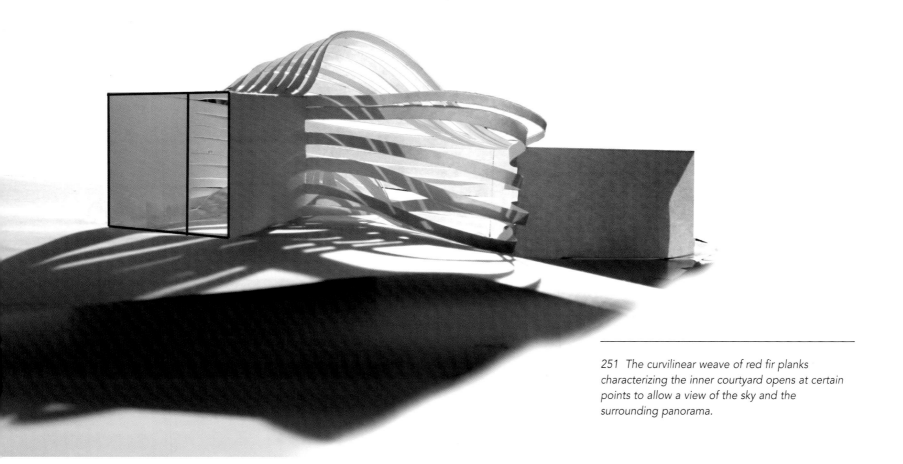

251 *The curvilinear weave of red fir planks characterizing the inner courtyard opens at certain points to allow a view of the sky and the surrounding panorama.*

252 top The inner courtyard is distributed over various levels, proposing itself as a sort of open-air living room, where one can pass time in the shade of the wooden pergola.

252 bottom The transparent wall delimiting the two rooms and facing toward the inner courtyard allows visual communication among the diverse elements of the module.

252-253 The contrast between the gray tones of the external shell and the warm tones of the interior coatings and the courtyard was obtained by treating the same material in different manners.

Ecological Children's Activity Center

KOH KOOD, THAILAND

A six-star eco-resort on Koh Kood island in Thailand has recently added to its guest services a series of activities for children, contained in an extraordinary structure the mere sight of which stimulates the imagination.

The project planners, taking inspiration from the tropical underwater panorama, designed a large bamboo cupola resembling a manta ray. Dominating the bay occupied by the resort and suspended above ground, this artificial organism seems ready to dive into the blue of the nearby sea.

Inside this shell, children can join in a series of activities specifically conceived to stimulate their environmental awareness, taking place in the cinema/auditorium and the four rooms designed as the "organs" of the structure. These are the library, containing a series of volumes on permaculture and local traditions, and three rooms dedicated to art, music, and fashion, where they can learn by playing. A sort of shell in which children can rest hangs from the structure. A cavern equipped with a vegetable garden is also available so they can prepare their own meals under the guidance of a cook.

The form of the structure respects the bioclimatic rules of tropical environments in order to keep the interior comfortable with minimum energy costs. The large cover, of organic form, was realized with an 8 m (about 25 ft) overhang, providing the required shade for the entire building as well as protection from torrential rains. The raised section was designed for maximum natural air circulation and an adequate level of natural lighting.

The most daunting challenge of the project to was to erect a building with natural and contemporary materials, using traditional local construction techniques. To achieve this goal, a close collaboration was necessary among the project planners, consultants coming from all parts of the world, experts in various disciplines, and a local team of craftsmen expert at building bamboo structures. The project required, first of all, the construction of a virtual model, followed by the realization of a 1:30 scale prototype, necessary not only to better define the behavior of the structural elements, but also to be able to test the structure in a wind tunnel.

254-255 The building hosts activities for children organized in the context of an exclusive ecological resort immersed in nature and facing onto the sea on the island of Koh Kood in Thailand.

Acting on the suggestion of one of the top experts in the use of bamboo, the structure was built with individual elements about 10 cm (about 4 in) in diameter, up to 9 m (about 30 ft) long, protected from insects with a coating based on boron salts. It was assembled at least 30 cm (about 12 in) above ground to avoid rising humidity, and protected from ultraviolet rays by means of the shade from the large cover.

The curved pieces were created by making use of a special steam oven created for the occasion.

The bearing elements made of bamboo, combined with elements of rattan, were plugged with the wood of a native species of eucalyptus used to make the floors. Bamboo sawdust was mixed with red earth to construct the walls, finished with white sand or wood splinters, depending on their orientation.   B.S.

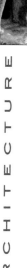
257 top and bottom In view of the complexity of the structural interweaving of the bamboo canes supporting the building, the project required construction of a virtual module to verify its static behavior.

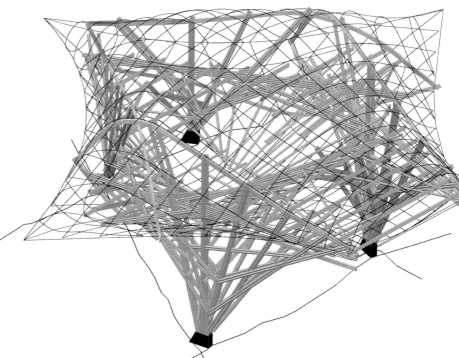

256-257 The structure recalls the form of a stingray about to dive into the facing blue sea. It is raised from the ground to facilitate maximum natural circulation of air inside.

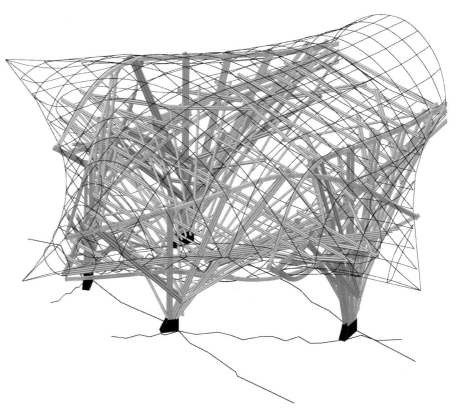

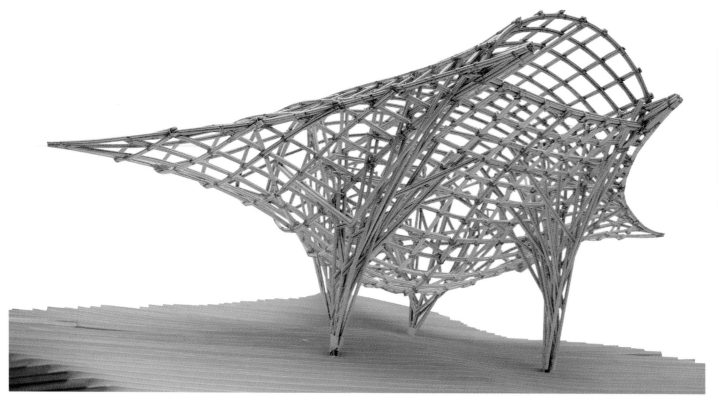

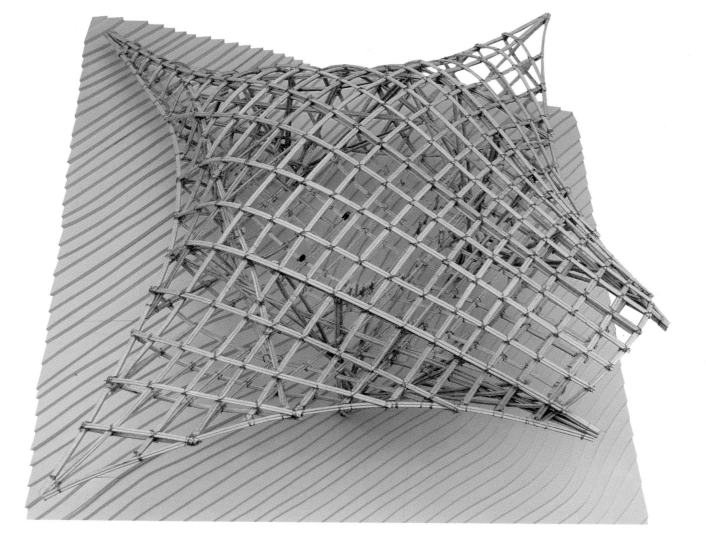

258 top and bottom The dynamic behavior of the structure was tested, particularly with reference to horizontal loads, in the wind tunnel using a 1:30 scale prototype.

258-259 top The bearing structure was built using native bamboo and realized with the collaboration of local craftsmen, who know perfectly well the secrets of this material.

258-259 bottom Each individual element made of bamboo required a steam treatment, which was effected on-site using an artisanal oven constructed specifically for the purpose.

259 bottom right Once the steam treatment was completed, each element was extracted from the large tube containing it and shaped to accord with the configuration required by the structure.

260-261 The entry walkway for the structure reveals the exclusive use of natural materials of local origin, assembled in accordance with traditional techniques.

260 bottom The mantle of the roof is covered with a series of shingles nailed onto a frame of wooden fillets, resting on the bamboo cupola.

261 The entire structure is
supported by a complex
interweaving of bamboo
elements, assembled according
to traditional techniques and
reinforced with steel connections
that are practically concealed.

262-263 The heart of the building is the amphitheater to entertain the young clients.

263 At the center of the large hall is a somewhat secluded corner, partly suspended, where the children, nestled among the colored cushions, can let fly their own fantasies.

264-265 Four different rooms have been fashioned around the amphitheater, illuminated by the natural light filtering through the openings that separate the various levels of the roof.

266 The structure is completely immersed in nature and even includes sanitary facilities reserved for the small ones, constructed in the form of a turtle.

267 top and bottom The "grotto" hosting the kitchen has an organic form recalling an imaginary animal. Here the children can prepare their own lunches under the guidance of a cook.

268 The interior of the structure built to allow the youngest guests to rest offers a tranquil and secluded environment that is also comfortable.

269 The building where the youngest children sleep was conceived as a particularly fantastical form, to make even the most capricious children want to enter.

BIBLIOGRAPHY

Aflalo, Marcelo et al., *Madeira como Estrutura. A história da ITA*, Paralaxe, São Paulo 2005.

Andi, Stefano, *Architettura organica vivente. Nascita, attualità e prospettive*, Esselibri - Edizioni Simone, Naples 2005.

Anger, Romain; Fontaine, Laetitia, *Bâtir en terre. Du grain de sable à l'architecture*, Editions Belin/ Cité des Sciences et de l'Industrie, Paris 2009.

Bahamón, Alejandro; Sanjinés María Camila, *ReMaterial*, Editorial Parramón, Barcelona 2008.

Berrini, Maria; Poggio, Andrea, *Green Life. Guida alla vita nelle città di domani*, Edizioni Ambiente, Milan 2010.

Bettini, Virginio, *Elementi di ecologia urbana*, Einaudi, Turin 1996.

Butera, Federico M., *Dalla caverna alla casa ecologica. Storia del comfort e dell'energia*, Edizioni Ambiente, Milan 2007.

Castelli, Luca, *Architettura sostenibile*, UTET Scienze Tecniche, Turin 2008.

Costa Duran, Sergi; Pohl, Ethel Baraona; Bollini, Liliana, *New Green Homes. The latest in sustainable living*, Harpercollins Publishers, London 2009.

Dall'Ò, Giuliano; Galante, Annalisa, *Abitare sostenibile*, Il Mulino, Bologna 2010.

de Botton, Alain, *Architettura e felicità*, Ugo Guanda Editore, Parma 2006.

Gauzin-Müller, Dominique, *Architettura sostenibile. 29 esempi europei di edifici e insediamenti ad alta qualità ambientale*, Edizioni Ambiente, Milan 2003.

Gauzin-Müller, Dominique, *Case ecologiche. I principi, le tendenze, gli esempi*, Edizioni Ambiente, Milan 2006.

Gauzin-Müller, Dominique, *Case in legno. La storia, le tecniche, gli esempi*, Edizioni Ambiente, Milan 2007.

Gauzin-Müller, Dominique, *L'architecture écologique du Vorarlberg*, Éditions du Moniteur, Paris 2009.

Gunter, Pauli, *Blue Economy. 10 anni, 100 innovazioni, 100 milioni di posti di lavoro*, Edizioni Ambiente, Milan 2010.

Jodidio, Philip, *Green Architecture Now!*, Taschen, Köln 2009.

Jones, Louise, *Environmentally Responsible Design: Green and Sustainable Design for Interior Designers*, John Wiley & Sons, Inc., Hoboken, N.J. 2008.

Manzini, Ezio; Jégou, François, *Quotidiano sostenibile. Scenari di vita urbana*, Edizioni Ambiente, Milan 2003.

Mostafavi, Mohsen (a cura di), *Ecological Urbanism*, Lars Müller Publishers, Baden 2010.

Risotti, Giuseppe, *Ambiente urbano. Introduzione all'ecologia urbana*, Dario Flaccovio Editore, Palermo 2007.

Sassi, Paola, *Strategie per l'architettura sostenibile. I fondamenti di un nuovo approccio al progetto*, Edizioni Ambiente, Milan 2007.

Schittich, Christian, *Architettura solare - Progettazione climatica per il XXI secolo*, Edition Detail - Birkhäuser, Munich 2004.

Vale, Robert; Vale, Brenda, *Time to eat the dog?*, Thames & Hudson, London 2009.

Various Authors, *Atlante della sostenibilità*, UTET, Turin 2007.

Various Authors, Actes Sud/Cité de l'architecture et du patrimoine, *Ecological Living*, Paris 2009.

Worldwatch Institute, *State of the World 2007*, W.W. Norton & Company, New York 2007.

INDEX

PHOTO CREDITS

Kambič, Miran pages 2-3, 46-47 top, 48-49, 49 top, 50 top, 50 bottom, 50-51

Karawitz Architecture, courtesy of, page 147 bottom

Klomfar, Bruno pages 84 bottom, 84-85, 85 top, 86 bottom, 86-87, 88-89, 89

Kon, Nelson pages 26-27, 28-29, 29 top, 66-67, 68-69, 70-71, 71 bottom

Koponen, Olavi, courtesy of, page 31 bottom, 32, 33 bottom, 188 top

Lobo, Pedro pages 208-209

Marcos Acayaba Arquitetos, courtesy of, pages 169 bottom, 172 top, 172 center, 172 bottom, 173 bottom, 174 center, 174 top, 174 bottom

Mareines+Patalano Arquitetura, courtesy of, pages 209 top, 210 top, 211 top, 211 center, 211 bottom, 212 bottom

Motte, Jean Louis page 118

Murcutt, Glenn, courtesy of, pages 20 top, 20-21, 21 bottom, 22 top, 22 bottom, 23, 24 bottom, 24-25 top, 25 bottom

mXarchitecture, courtesy of, pages 218 top, 219 bottom, 220 center, 220 bottom

Nitsche Arquitetos Associados, courtesy of, pages 26 bottom, 27 bottom, 28 top

Nolan, Nancy pages 154 top, 154-155 top, 156 top, 156 bottom, 157

Pablo Katz Architecture, courtesy of, pages 90 bottom, 92 bottom, 93 top, 93 bottom, 96 bottom

Panchee, Kiattipong, courtesy of 24H

architecture, pages 254-255, 260-261, 260 bottom, 261, 262-263

Rintala, Sami, courtesy of, page 135

Rintala Eggertsson Architects, courtesy of, pages 130, 132, 133 top, 133 bottom, 134 top

Rinuccini, Arnaud, courtesy of Pablo Katz Architecture, pages 90 top, 91, 92 top, 94 top, 94-95, 95 bottom, 96 top, 97

Riolzi, Paolo pages 228-229, 230-231 top, 232 bottom, 232-233, 236 bottom, 236-237 top

Ryntovt Design, courtesy of, pages 240-241, 241 top, 242, 242-243, 244, 244-245

Sarah Wigglesworth Architects, courtesy of, pages 184 top right, 185 top, 185 center, 185 bottom

Sarah Wigglesworth & Jeremy Till, courtesy of, pages 182 top, 182 bottom, 183 top, 183 bottom

Sigurjónsson, Sigurgeir, courtesy of Studio Granda Architects, pages 142 top, 142-143, 144, 144-145

SINGLE Speed DESIGN (SsD), courtesy of, pages 9, 122 bottom, 122-123, 123 bottom, 124 top, 124 bottom, 124-125, 126, 127, 128, 128 top, 129

Smoothy, Paul pages 180 bottom left, 180 bottom right, 180-181, 184 bottom left

Sobek, Werner, courtesy of, pages 104 left, 104-105 bottom, 106 top right, 106 center, 108-109, 110 top, 110 center, 110 bottom

Sou Fujimoto Architects, courtesy of, pages 200 bottom, 201 bottom, 202 top

Studio Granda Architects, courtesy of, pages 142 bottom, 143 bottom

Studio Mumbai Architects, courtesy of, pages 58 bottom left, 60 bottom, 60-61, 61 bottom, 62 top, 62 bottom, 62-63, 63 bottom, 65 bottom

Swimmer, Lara page 114, 115, 116 top

Thun, Matteo, courtesy of, pages 228, 229 bottom, 230 top, 230-231 bottom, 232 top, 233 top, 234 top, 234 bottom

Tiainen, Jussi, courtesy of Olavi Koponen, pages 4-5, 30-31 top, 30-31 bottom, 32-33, 34, 35, 36-37, 38-39, 39, 186 left center, 186 left bottom, 186-187, 188 bottom, 188-189, 190 top, 190 bottom, 191

Ulin, Pia pages 131, 134 bottom right

Unterrainer, Walter, courtesy of, pages 112 top, 112 bottom, 113 top, 113 bottom

Vigilius Mountain Resort, courtesy of, pages 234 center, 235, 237 bottom

Weintraub, Alan/Arcaid page 28 bottom

Werner Tscholl Architekt, courtesy of, pages 162 top, 162-163, 163 bottom, 164-165, 165 top, 165 bottom, 166 top, 166 center left, 166 center right, 166 bottom, 166-167

Wherrett, Jonathan pages 78-79, 80-81 top, 82 top, 82-83, 83 bottom

Zeisser, Boris, courtesy of 24H architecture, pages 256-257, 263, 264-265, 266, 267 top, 267 bottom, 268, 269

Zen Architects, courtesy of, pages 52 top, 56 bottom, 138 right, 140 bottom

ACKNOWLEDGEMENTS

The Publisher would like to thank:

24H architecture, Rotterdam: Olav Bruin, Mirjam van der Linde and Boris Zeisser

albordE arquitectos, Quito: David Barragán and Pascual Gangotena

Andrade Morettin Arquitetos, São Paulo: Marina Rosenfeld Snelwar

Architecture Foundation Australia, Brooklyn: Lindsay Johnston

Architectuurbureau Sluijmer en van Leeuwen, Utrecht: Hans Sluijmer and Wouter van Riet Paap

Pieta-Linda Auttila, Helsinki

baumraum, Brema: Andreas Wenning

Pietro Carmine

Davide Macullo Architects, Lugano: Aileen Forbes-Munnelly

Dietrich Untertrifaller Architekten, Bregenz: Judith Wellmann

Dock4 Architecture, Hobart: Michael Shrapnel

Donnet Tresse Architectes, Nantes: Olivier Donnet

Ecosistema Urbano, Madrid: Domenico Di Siena, Michael Moradiellos, Belinda Tato and José Luis Vallejo

Emma Doherty & Amanda Menage, London: Amanda Menage

EXiT architetti associati, Treviso: Giuseppe Pagano

Fabienne Gérin-Jean, Paris: Fabienne Gérin-Jean and Annabelle Verrecchia

Alessio Guarino, Tokyo

Michael Hughes, Sharjah

Hiroshi Iguchi, Tokyo

HyBrid Architecture, Seattle: Joel Egan

Karawitz Architecture, Paris: Caroline Delbarre

Olavi Koponen, Helsinki

Marcos Acayaba Arquitetos, São Paulo: Marcos Acayaba

Mareines+Patalano Arquitetura, Rio de Janeiro: Julia Queima

Kayano Matsumoto, Tokyo

Glenn Murcutt, Mosman

mXarchitecture, Paris: Emmanuel Choupis

Nitsche Arquitetos Associados, São Paulo: Lua Nitsche, Rafael Baravelli and Natassia Caldas

Pablo Katz Architecture, Paris: Laurent Chapuis

Rintala Eggertsson Architects, Bodø: Sami Rintala

Ryntovt Design, Kharkov: Yuriy Ryntovt and Ksenia Yeloyeva

Sarah Wigglesworth Architects, London: Eleanor Brough

SINGLE Speed DESIGN (SsD), New York-Cambridge, MA: F. Peter Ortner

Werner Sobek, Stuttgart: Frank Heinlein

Sou Fujimoto Architects, Tokyo: Kanna Arita and Aya Tatsuta

Studio Aisslinger, Berlin: Verena Stella Gompf

Studio Granda Architects, Reykjavik: Steve Christer

Studio Mumbai Architects, Mumbai: Samuel Barclay and Vatsal Vekaria

Matteo Thun, Milan: Daniela Artuso

Werner Tscholl Architekt, Morter: Werner Tscholl

Jussi Tiainen, Helsinki

Walter Unterrainer, Feldkirch

UPM-Kymmene and wisa24.com

Vigilius Mountain Resort, Lana

Zen Architects, Melbourne: Riccardo Zen, Erika Bartak and Ben Callery

WS White Star Publishers® is a registered trademark property of Edizioni White Star s.r.l.

© 2011 Edizioni White Star s.r.l.
Via Candido Sassone, 24
13100 Vercelli, Italy
www.whitestar.it

Translation: John Venerella
Editing: Suzanne Smither

ISBN 978-88-544-0594-3
1 2 3 4 5 6   15 14 13 12 11

Printed in Italy